SEMEIA 60

FANTASY AND THE BIBLE

Guest Editors:
George Aichele and Tina Pippin

©1992
by the Society of Biblical Literature

SEMEIA 60

Copyright © 1992 by the Society of Biblical Literature

All rights reserved. No part of this work may be reproduced or transmitted in any form or by any means, electronic or mechanical, including photocopying and recording, or by means of any information storage or retrieval system, except as may be expressly permitted by the 1976 Copyright Act or in writing from the publisher. Requests for permission should be addressed in writing to the Rights and Permissions Office, Society of Biblical Literature, 825 Houston Mill Road, Atlanta, GA 30329, USA.

ISSN 0095-571X
ISBN 1-58983-140-3

Printed in the United States of America
on acid-free paper

CONTENTS

Contributors to this Issue VI

Introduction: Why the Fantastic? 1
    George Aichele
    Tina Pippin

1. The Messianic Power of Fantasy in the Bible 7
    Jack Zipes

2. Prototypic Horror: The Genre of the Book of Job 23
    Roger Schlobin

3. Biblical Narrative and Categories of the Fantastic 39
    Peter D. Miscall

4. The Fantastic in the Discourse of Jesus 53
    George Aichele

5. The Heroine and the Whore:
    Fantasy and the Female in the Apocalypse of John 67
    Tina Pippin

6. Response: Fantasy and the New Testament 83
    Joanna Dewey

7. The Bible in Fantasy 91
    Colin Manlove

8. Prophetic and Apocalyptic Eschatology
    in Ursula Le Guin's *The Farthest Shore* and *Tehanu* 111
    Mara Donaldson

9. Additional Bibliography 123

CONTRIBUTORS TO THIS ISSUE

George Aichele
   Department of Philosophy/Religion
   Adrian College
   110 S. Madison Street
   Adrian, MI 49221-2575

Joanna Dewey
   Episcopal Divinity School
   99 Brattle Street
   Cambridge, MA 02138

Mara Donaldson
   Department of Religion
   Dickinson College
   Carlisle, PA 17013-2896

Colin Manlove
   Department of English Literature
   University of Edinburgh
   David Hume Tower
   George Square
   Edinburgh EH8 9JX
   SCOTLAND

Peter Miscall
   Saint Thomas Theological Seminary
   1300 South Steele Street
   Denver, CO 80210-2599

Tina Pippin
   Department of Bible and Religion
   Agnes Scott College
   Decatur, GA 30030

Roger C. Schlobin
   Department of English
   Purdue University—North Central
   Westville, IN 46391

Jack Zipes
   Department of German
   University of Minnesota
   219 Folwell Hall, 9 Pleasant St. SE
   Minneapolis, MN 55455-02123

INTRODUCTION: WHY THE FANTASTIC?

George Aichele
Tina Pippin

1. *The Significance of Fantasy.*

> [P]oetry is more philosophical and serious business than history; for poetry speaks more of universals, history of particulars. "Universal" in this case is what kind of person is likely to do or say certain things, according to probability or necessity; that is what poetry aims at ... (Aristotle, *Poetics*:51b5–10)

> One should, on the other hand, choose events that are impossible but plausible in preference to ones that are possible but implausible; but on the other hand, one's plots should not be made up of irrational incidents.... But if one does put them in and they are "gotten across" to the listener in more or less convincing fashion, even an absurdity can be tolerated. (60a27–28, 34–35)

Aristotle apparently disapproved of the fantastic. Given the stress that he places on mimesis as a crucial feature of "poetry," this is not surprising. Nevertheless, he clearly leaves room for the nonreal in narrative, provided that it does not overly strain the audience's credulity. Plato, on the other hand, often made his hero Socrates tell fanciful stories in order to make dialectical points. Perhaps such stories (such as the Myth of Theuth in the *Phaedrus*) were not as implausible to Plato's readers (or to Socrates) as they are to us. However, Plato believed that literary mimesis and the beliefs which it arouses are dangerous and delusive, as he makes clear in the *Republic*.

One can hardly begin to read literary theory, or philosophy, without encountering remarks on the fantastic. For instance, René Descartes paid a great deal of attention to his dreams, and these dreams play important roles in his arguments. Thomas Hobbes was also troubled by his inability to explain how he could distinguish between dreams and waking, even though the distinction itself was not usually difficult to make. Following Hobbes, the British empiricists developed theories of cognition in which "fancy" and the imagination had significant roles to play. David Hume's views on the matter influenced Immanuel Kant and were transformed by Kant into a theory of aesthetics which was echoed and developed further, once again specifically in relation to literary works, by Samuel Taylor Coleridge. In the twentieth century, phenomenologists such as Gaston Bachelard, Roman Ingarden, and Hans–Georg Gadamer have continued to pursue these questions.

Yet running through this entire history (of which the above is the merest of sketches) are two questions, which for lack of a clear answer have both confused the issue and often (but not always) relegated fantasy theory to a matter of secondary importance, a subject not to be taken quite seriously. First, what is the relation (or the difference) between fantasy as a mental or psychological phenomenon on the one hand, and fantasy as a narrative feature or structure on the other? Surely there are important differences between a cognitive experience and a literary genre. What are these differences? Do these two uses of the one word implicate one another? Would we be interested in fantastic stories if we could not fantasize? Does fantasy literature consist of personal fantasies which have been written down? Or do we have to be taught how to fantasize—perhaps by hearing or reading fantastic stories? Is this the function for children of fairy tales and nursery rhymes?

The fact that we use "fantasy" to refer to both mental and literary phenomena should not be allowed to obscure the differences between these two types of phenomena. Unfortunately, however, a great deal of theory and criticism slips almost unconsciously back and forth between these poles, and to the extent that the distinction is never clarified, the value of that theory and that criticism is restricted. This slippage may be particularly dangerous to the study of the Bible as fantasy. For the most part, what we are concerned with in the present volume is the study of narrative form, and not of the mental state of the Bible's authors or readers.

The second question is, what is the relation (or connection) between fantasy and reality? In order to avoid committing the fault which we have just noted, let us restrict ourselves to literary fantasy, meaning recorded narratives which somehow deserve the name of "fantasy." Are fantastic stories merely opposite in some way to "realistic" stories—those narratives which (to a greater or lesser degree) imitate what we understand the "real world" to be? In other words, do fantasies merely modify one or more of the "ground rules" of consensual reality? Fantasy then would be a sort of peripheral genre, spun off from the main streams of literature by a simple process of polar reversal. What one generation or culture regarded as fantasy might not be so regarded by another.

Most theories of fantasy take this approach, although for the better (more interesting, more sophisticated) theories, the spin–off process is by no means simple. For these theories, fantasy provides a sort of escape from reality, which might be quite therapeutic, or even salvific. ("Escapism" is not always bad!)

Other theoretical strategies are also possible. For classical Marxism, fantasy like religion was utopian and therefore counterrevolutionary;

however, following the lead especially of Ernst Bloch, neo-Marxist scholars such as Rosemary Jackson have reconsidered literary fantasy (at least in its utopian forms) as the potential for envisioning an "other world," a place or state of being which grants to those who can enter it the power to change the real world. Here the fantastic is once again determined in large part by reality, but it contains within itself the power to produce real transformations of the world—fantasy is not an escape from reality.

Yet another alternative is presented by poststructuralist thinkers, building on hints and traces in the writings of Roland Barthes, Jacques Lacan, and others, for whom the fantastic is intrinsic to the structure of language and literature. Fantasy, according to these theorists, is the point at which the artifice and, ultimately, the fictionality of every signifying system is revealed for what it is. Reality loses its primacy in this view, and our understanding of reality is in fact produced through and determined by the suppression of the fantastic.

These theoretical distinctions have a way of blurring and blending together in the actual analyses of specific texts. It is not the goal of this volume to resolve these thorny and perhaps unsolvable theoretical differences. However, it is important to keep them in mind, especially as it becomes clear in these essays that fantasy theory is not one simple, clear-cut thing.

2. Fantasy Theory and Biblical Studies.

A dialogue has been developing in recent years in both the American Academy of Religion and the Society of Biblical Literature between theology and biblical studies on the one hand and studies in fantasy theory and literature on the other. We hope that this issue of *Semeia* will give added impetus to this dialogue and will be a step toward future scholarship in literary fantasy and the Bible.

Tzvetan Todorov outlined three conditions necessary for fantastic literature: readers must hesitate in their identification with the hero; readers "hesitate between a natural and a supernatural explanation of the events described"; and readers must reject both allegorical and poetic readings of the text (1973:32–34). Rosemary Jackson expands on Todorov's definition and proposes that "[f]antasy re-combines and inverts the real, but it does not escape it: it exists in a parasitical or symbiotic relation to the real. The fantastic cannot exist independently of that 'real' world which it seems to find so frustratingly finite" (20). Jack Zipes argues that the "liberating magic" of traditional fairy tales "is not ethereal hocus pocus but the real symbolic potential of the tales to designate ways for creating what Ernst Bloch calls concrete utopias in the here and now" (1984:xi). These definitions point to the connection of the genre of the fantastic with several biblical genres (such as myth and heroic legend, wisdom and apocalyptic literature, and parable and gospel).

The goal of this volume is to introduce biblical scholars to the outlines and fundamental concepts of selected contemporary theories of literary fantasy and to demonstrate the application of these concepts to biblical texts. While the central theoretical focus of the volume is defined in relation to contemporary views such as those of Todorov, Jackson, and Zipes, more traditional views—such as those of Coleridge and, more recently, J. R. R. Tolkien—are not excluded. The contrasts between these views are not only mutually illuminating, but also illuminative of larger narratological and text-theoretical issues, including those of political and feminist readings. Much of the controversy that occupies contemporary secular literary (and biblical) studies—between the modern and the postmodern, concerning the status and authority of the text, of the reader, of the canon, etc.—can be further clarified in relation to fantasy theory and literature. Fantasy studies are particularly useful in uncovering the codes of a text—of gender, ideology, anthropology, utopia, etc.—because fantasy arises in tension with belief.

3. *Acknowledgements/Contributors.*

The editors express their particular gratitude to the contributors to this volume. Because this multidisciplinary dialogue is so new, very few scholars are well versed in both the studies of literary fantasy and of the biblical literatures. The authors involved in this project reflect a wide variety of disciplines and orientations. There are agreements and disagreements and different biases and agendas represented. On the fantasy side, we approached many scholars and writers with the idea for this volume and received interesting responses: from famous authors who graciously replied that they had to finish their next novel, to fantasy theorists who had "dropped out" of academics to become fantasy writers, to the fantasy theorists who agreed to share their ideas. The experience of initiating this discourse on fantasy and the Bible was risky but positive.

The willingness of the authors and, indeed, their enthusiasm in attempting to bridge what is at present a large and daunting chasm has been heartening to us. We are also very grateful to Robert Culley and the editorial board of *Semeia* for their interest in and willingness to undertake this project. Finally, we thank the members of the International Association for Fantasy in Art and Literature (IAFA) for their involvement in conference sessions on "Fantasy in the Bible/The Bible in Fantasy" during 1991 and 1992, where we were able to try out some of the ideas presented here.

Jack Zipes has studied traditional German fairy tales as well as contemporary fantasy writings and films in works such as *Breaking the Magic Spell, The Brothers Grimm: From Enchanted Forests to the Modern World*, and *Spells of Enchantment: The Wondrous Fairy Tales of Western Culture*. In "The Messianic Power of Fantasy in the Bible," Zipes begins with a discussion of Bloch's theory of the fantastic as a principle of hope and then summarizes his own views, indicating the place they occupy in contemporary fantasy theory, and discussing their relevance to biblical studies, including feminism and political theory.

Roger Schlobin is editor of *The Aesthetics of Fantasy Literature and Art*, general editor of the widely-used "Starmont Guides" to fantasy and science fiction literature, and author of numerous bibliographies on this topic. In "Prototypic Horror: The Genre of the Book of Job," Schlobin argues that a comparison of the characteristics of Job to those of modern works reveals it to be a prototype for Jewish and Christian concepts of fear and terror and their manifestations, as the "dark inversion of signs, symbols, and expectations," in modern literature.

In addition to serving as editors of this volume, George Aichele and Tina Pippin have contributed articles extending their respective current work on fantasy and the New Testament. In "The Fantastic in the Discourse of Jesus," Aichele examines selected dialogues and longer discourses of Jesus, drawing largely upon Todorov's theory of the fantastic, and he argues that the earliest strata of the gospel traditions reveal a dimension of the fantastic in material which is obscured and neutralized in later strata. In "The Heroine and the Whore: Fantasy and the Female in the Apocalypse of John," Pippin claims that the representation of female characters and symbols in the Apocalypse reveals the misogyny and patriarchy of that text, which thereby controls erotic power and excludes the female from the utopian vision of the New Jerusalem.

Peter Miscall and Joanna Dewey are well-known to biblical scholars for their studies of narrative structures of the Hebrew Scriptures and of the New Testament, respectively. Miscall examines the ten plagues of Exodus 1-15 as miracles combining human and divine power. Dewey responds to the articles by Aichele and Pippin and reflects on the larger issues of the discourse of fantasy theory and New Testament studies.

Modern Fantasy: Five Studies, by Colin Manlove, is one of the major recent statements of fantasy theory. Manlove has presently completed a book entitled *Christian Fantasy: From Twelve Hundred to the Present*. In "The Bible in Fantasy," he considers the relation of recent fantasy literature to the Bible as located and moving between two differing possibilities: sacramental participation (Tolkien), or mediation/translation of the holy into the secular (Moltmann, Jaspers).

Mara Donaldson has previously explored theological dimensions of contemporary "secular" literary fantasy. In "Prophetic and Apocalyptic Eschatology in Ursula Le Guin's *The Farthest Shore* and *Tehanu*," Donaldson considers the use of biblical imagery and concepts in contemporary fantasy writings by women. She examines the apparent dualism of apocalyptic in terms of the role it plays in sustaining the radical impropriety of injustice or evil in a good world.

THE MESSIANIC POWER OF FANTASY IN THE BIBLE

Jack Zipes
University of Minnesota

ABSTRACT

Ernst Bloch's reading of the Bible at the end of *The Principle of Hope* raises important ideological questions of the Bible as fantasy literature. To understand "the messianic power of fantasy" in the Bible the reader must be a detective, encountering the text as an unsolvable mystery. This Marxist approach to fantasy emphasizes the material relationships that are basic to the discontent of the oppressed with the status quo. Fantasy subverts in its utopian vision, which is determined by its *Vor-Schein* or anticipatory illumination that leads the oppressed from darkness to the light of hope.

---

1. Introduction.

The idea of the Messiah has survived only in its biblical form; only in this form was it experienced by peoples with suffering and a sense of mission. And because it expressed that which constitutes the essence of religious longing, with astral-mythic statics set aside, with all the after-ripening of the exodus god, it is plagiarism, though plagiarism, not just of Persia but of the central utopia of religions themselves. Every founder of a religion appeared in an aura *which belongs to the Messiah*, and every foundation of a religion has, as glad tidings, *the new heaven, the new earth on the horizon*, even when both perfectednesses have been abused by the masters' churches for the idealization, i.e. apologetics of an existing order.

(Ernst Bloch, *The Principle of Hope*)

The Bible is the seminal work of all fantasy literature.[1] While seemingly providing a world order through a narrative about the origins of the universe and the events that lead, in the Old and New Testament, to the foundation of a Judeo-Christian morality, it subverts this order with promises of other worlds/other spaces. The Bible transports us back in time to a legendary past to encourage us to look forward (out of dissatisfaction with the present) to another and better world. The Bible undermines reality and will not let us rest content with conditions as they are. And like all great works of fantasy it provides us with the hope that the other, or what Ernst Bloch calls, "the utterly different," is possible.

Alterity is key to fantasy, the extraordinary in the ordinary, the explosiveness of the miraculous, that enables us to set our sights realistically on a promised land, otherwise we are left with false promises. The Bible does not leave us with false promises. Institutions do. Professions and professionals do. Canons do. Religions do. The Bible must be taken out of context. Re-turned to and into fantasy.

a. *Bloch and the Bible.*

It is not by chance that Ernst Bloch, the Marxist philosopher who wrote about atheism in Christianity, devoted the latter part of his major work *The Principle of Hope* to the Bible. Bloch was always trying to read the Bible as a detective reading a mystery for clues not about the solution to a crime but about the nature of the miraculous. In this sense the Bible is authentic mystery, which gives secular fantasy its meaning, and we as readers must be detectives. Bloch explains:

> The purpose of detective reading would have to involve revelation of *the most positive things* that would come from the discovering and dismantling of Ezra's editing of the Bible and from the preservation of the submerged 'plebeian' elements in the Bible. Of course, they are only submerged to a certain extent. Otherwise the Bible would have the same effect as any other book of religion of the upper class and of idolized despotism instead of representing the most revolutionary book of religion ever, itself irrepressible, thanks to the power of its antithesis that continually creates space: *the son of man—Egypt land*. Textual criticism that refers to this antithesis cannot in any way be neutral like, for example, Homer criticism. Rather, this antithesis (*nemo audit nisi spiritu libertatis intus docente*) gives philology a goal. (1977a:103-04)

Bloch insists that all reading is intentional, but the reading that is most intentionally suited to the Bible is one that opens it up as a mystery. Therefore, the Bible calls for detective reading, informed by revolutionary hope, for the Bible is intentional in its anticipatory illumination of the promised land, its exodus from oppression in Egypt, from Moses to Jesus, from the desert to building a paradise on earth. The intent is determined by human aspiration, daydreams, glowing forth. Traditional textual criticism has intentionally and unintentionally blurred the utopian landscape of the Bible, the traces that enable us to glimpse the potential we have of humanizing nature and making ourselves more natural. The Bible projects light from ourselves back upon ourselves. This is what the crowd learns in John's Gospel:

> "We have heard from the law that the Messiah remains forever. How can you say that the Son of Man must be lifted up? Who is this Son of man?" Jesus said to them, "The light is with you a little longer. Walk while you have the light, so that the darkness may not overtake you. If you walk in the darkness,

you do not know where you are going. While you have the light, believe in the light, so that you may become children of the light." (12:34-36)

In *The Principle of Hope* and other writings, Bloch seeks to recuperate the messianic power of fantasy in the Bible that is connected to the light of anticipatory illumination. A suggestive reading of Bloch reading the Bible offers possibilities to comprehend the key role the Bible plays in the development of fantasy literature—and also to determine criteria for fantasy. After all, much of what we call fantasy is hallucinatory. Certainly not good for the head. But also not good for the stomach. Good fantasy gives you something to chew on. There is no fantasy without materiality.

Bloch seeks to ground the Bible in humanity and materiality in *The Principle of Hope* paradoxically so that it will inspire us to fly. In his reading of the Bible he focuses time and again on Moses and Jesus as symbolical figures representing humankind's *exodus*—the rebellion against despotism, the moving out to experiment and explore in search of the promised land, which is both a penetration into God and voyage toward realizing the divine in humanity. All religions have their own utopian symbolism, but Bloch places greatest emphasis on the Judeo-Christian images in the Bible because their *intentionality* is connected to an enlightened view of the world that seeks to clarify the ontological situation of humankind. Bloch relates:

> Judaism already posits the religion of exodus; Christianity with an anthropological critique of religion, as it were, represents the son of man at the dawn of the kingdom without father idols, with the genesis not as beginning, rather as apocalyptical end. All religions have a kind of invariable final symbol at bottom, different as well as contrary in imagination and appearance because they are socially determined, and therefore, ideological. However, they also contribute to utopian formation. But the explicitness of the intention of the symbol itself does not change due to this. It is only directed toward the essence of the symbol that is still to come, and it is only for its sake that the intention of the symbol rises and senses what is to come. (1977b:207)

For Bloch, religion is an evolutionary process of human self-awareness that leads down from the heavens into the materiality of human nature and nature. The formation of the Jewish religion was a departure from what he termed pagan and *astral* religions and myths—astral because the gods were above, beyond the reach of human beings. With Judaism, according to Bloch, humans brought God to earth, and under the instigation of Moses, began a quest for the Messiah and promised land. The result from human imagination and social determination was the conception of Jesus Christ as the Messiah and *Menschensohn* (son of man),[2] pointing the way toward salvation and paradise. In this respect, there is no closure in the Bible; the end is the beginning. The Bible is a book of signs that leaves distinct utopian traces (*Spuren*) which readers still have to follow and make more concrete. Reading is the perception and recognition of messianic and apocalyptic signs:

> It was not without reason that the apocalyptic character made the Bible precisely into the instigator of revolutions. This can be seen most clearly in the German Peasants' War. It was not only the pathos of the Bible that serves this purpose as intended Glad Tidings for those who labor and are heavy laden but just as much its perspective of death and the life to come, the realization and completion of the *characters*, especially their dramatic actions, occurs in art, and its allegories intend in anticipatory illumination a transformation of the world without it ending. (1977b: 211)

3. *The Vor-Schein.*

As can be seen thus far, Bloch sought to make religion and the Bible the cornerstones of his revision of Marxism, while employing Marxist categories to read the Bible as mystery, but a mystery that is the foundation and instigation of all "good" fantasy. Such an unusual endeavor was crucial for the development of his aesthetics of anticipatory illumination (*Vor-Schein*). In his critical study of Bloch's philosophy, Wayne Hudson (184) comments:

> Bloch's originality is to interpret the counter-factual excess of religion as secretly wise, and as potentially constitutive for theory-praxis. Religion, Bloch argues, is full of utopianism and where there is hope, there is religion. What was intended by the great religions was absolute or total hope. Consistent with this view, Bloch argues that Marxism needs a new praxis-oriented approach to religion which actively inherits the symbolic pre-appearance [*Vor-Schein*, also translated as anticipatory illumination][3] found in religious history of mankind. Such an inheritance requires a Marxist critique of the ideology and illusion present in religious projections, which relates such projections to the development of classes and to particular modes of production. But it also requires a hermeneutic of the 'act content' such projections contain, which cannot be appropriated in any simplistic ideology free form. Instead, for Bloch, there is a translation of the genuine intentionality which the religious imagination of mankind has uncovered into a revolutionary socialist ideology which aims at theory praxis in the long run.

Implicit if not explicit in Bloch's philosophy is that, if one seeks and learns to read the signs of anticipatory illumination in the Bible and genuine biblical signs in fantasy literature, the reader will simultaneously be formed as a potential revolutionary in the process. True fantasy literature then is explosive and revolutionary. But here it is necessary to clarify Bloch's notions of anticipatory illumination, heritage, and messianism before we can grasp the relationship between the Bible and "true" fantasy literature.

Throughout Bloch's writings there is an underlying argument that there cannot be a *genuine* culture until society becomes classless. That is, Bloch's concept of cultural heritage (*Kulturerbe*) signifies that *heritage* is a process, the act of inheriting (*erben*), and that the qualitative act of inheriting as an unfinished process is what constitutes the value of culture that is on its way to becoming genuine. Since the framework for *acting*, for choosing what is to be inherited, has always been set by hegemonic groups in hierarchical societies, established culture has been exclusive. At the same time, its exclusivity and richness have relied on its "revolutionary" capacity to absorb and integrate whatever the subordinate classes have produced that is indelible (*unausgegolten*). Moreover, their demands for more access to the cultural goods (*Kulturgut*) and the surplus that they themselves produce have become part and parcel of capitalism over the centuries. Such a condition led Bloch to focus on the dialectical relationship between upper and lower classes, to analyze forms by which the upper sought to dominate and preserve its power, and the forms by which the lower aimed to subvert the domination of the upper and to gain self-awareness.

This political stance prompted Bloch to try to retrieve the neglected traces and submerged meanings of popular culture that lent substance to the development of high culture while also providing impetus for change. The telos of culture, the end toward which the cultural heritage would lead, as Bloch saw it, was the naturalization of human beings and the humanization of nature. Such a goal has not always been consciously viewed by the subordinate classes—or any class for that matter—and it will not be reached according to mechanical laws of history. Nor is culture the property of one particular class. Bloch constantly asserted that the qualitative advancement of genuine culture depended on the active desire of individuals to know themselves and to decide upon the designation of home (*Heimat*) for themselves. The order of the world was to be cultivated by autonomous subjects who were collectively to ascertain the beacons of light that anticipated the way to the classless society in which the *Kitsch* (junk, delusion) of capitalist production gives way to the concrete utopia in the amalgamation of high and low culture.

The starting point for Bloch is the *potential* autonomous subject or the *potential* productive reader as detective or detector. As individuals, we must solve the mystery of our lives, detect those signs that illuminate the way to ourselves. For Bloch:

> 'We are subjects without names, Kasper Hauser[4] natures, who drive with unknown direction and have still not unravelled these natures.' Thus the human being is here understood and designated as something that is still basically and directly in the dark, not even in the present at all and precisely because of this has history. The human being finds itself still on a journey with his/her entire world. The *ordre* has not been determined anywhere, however in the journey of self-discovery it is capable of possibly being illuminated, of first being represented in any way. (1974a:32)

The capacity of the individual to journey and to discover is a given for Bloch, but this does not mean that each individual will break out of the everyday routine to journey, or that each individual will really experience the chiliastic meaning of the journey, or that each individual will recognize the *Vor-Schein*, which indicates the way toward the humanization of nature and the naturalization of humans. Bloch (1974a:45) further remarks: "Unfortunately even the people (*Volk*) are not always so loyal and true. The longer time goes by, the more they understand *Kitsch* very well. They fall for it and are capable of being deceived with it and even increase on their side the petty-bourgeois job for it." In opposition to this, Bloch insists that the task for all readers and consumers of culture is to remain open to the *Not-Yet-Conscious* (*Noch-Nicht-Bewußte*) that will enable them to realize the *Not-Yet-Become* (*Noch-Nicht-Gewordene*). "The concept of the Not-Yet-Conscious enables the unconscious to be removed from the mere negation of consciousness and to differentiate in it clearly traces of memory and traces of hope, two completely distinct act-content-references (which only later can disappear after a conceptual differentiation, in parts also in their limitation [compare romanticism, archetypes]). But Not-Yet-Conscious with *Novum*5 only lies above, at the front of consciousness; a pre-conscious that does not remember but is auroratic (*aurorisch*) in which something new psychologically announces itself or anticipates itself" (1974b:115).

The obstacles preventing people from grasping the *Not-Yet-Conscious* emanate from a class-dominated cultural production that diverts and confuses the minds of people so that their imaginings of a new and better world are blurred, blocked, or perverted. Bloch investigated the *Schein*, the false illusion, of magazine stories, true romances, marathon dance contests, white-collar pretense, glittering Hollywood films, the Nazification of Germanic legends, rituals, and symbols, and many other forms of *Kitsch* to demonstrate how the tendency toward the genuine new (*Novum*) was often sidetracked in the interests of capitalism to make the status quo and even the regressive social forces appear fulfilling and invigorating. The only way to counter false illusions that reinforce capitalist rationalization and state bureaucratic control is to create and promote social movements that subvert and problematize the depictions of harmony and totality while conserving the cultural tendencies that awaken and sharpen the Not-Yet-Conscious. In the process a profound appreciation of the *Vor-Schein* must be developed if people are to realize their own interests and come out of the darkness into light, enlightened but not in a rationally instrumental manner. Rather, enlightenment for Bloch is connected to the fantastic projections realized in the Bible but have not been fully transposed into cultural practice for and by the people. We are confronted everywhere with *Vor-Schein*, that challenges us to transpose it, to become at one with its light.

As Gert Ueding has remarked, the category of *Vor-Schein* is related to the producer as well as to the artwork that is produced: "The Not-Yet-Become of the object manifests itself in the artwork as that which seeks itself, illuminates itself in advance in its meaning. With this, anticipatory illumination is not simply objective in contrast to subjective illusion. Rather, anticipatory illumination is the way of being that wakens utopian consciousness on its part and indicates to consciousness the Not-Yet-Become in the scale of its possibilities" (1974a:21). Thus, what determines the quality of the anticipatory illumination (and its utopian function as well) of a given work will be the artistic impulse and sensitivity along with the social vision behind it. For Bloch the "I" of the producer was inconceivable without the "We" of the producer's humanitarian vision. He conceived of works with anticipatory illumination as classless and non-ideological. That is, they spoke to people of all classes and did not bind themselves to one ideological position. In addition, works with anticipatory illumination were to be found in oral as well as literate societies, in all sorts of artifacts as well as social attitudes and customs. Greek and Roman art, Mozart's *Figaro*, Goethe's *Faust*, travel books of the 16th-18th centuries, Beethoven's *Ninth Symphony*, Hoffmann's *The Golden Flower Pot*, Gottfried Keller's *Green Henry*, the fairy tales of the Brothers Grimm, Karl May's westerns, detective novels, romances, science fiction, adventure stories, the circus, country fairs, fashion, architecture—these are just some of the products and phenomena which Bloch explored to locate anticipatory illumination in culture.

Certain criteria appear time and again in Bloch's designation of what constitutes *Vor-Schein*. For instance, in the fairy tale the anticipatory illumination is constituted by the manner in which the small hero uses cunning and courage to overcome obstacles and to defeat powerful oppressors. The protagonist's triumph signals a revolutionary triumph, an example of the underdog's potential to take charge of his or her life. The miraculous transformations in fairy tales reveal that life is a process of qualitative change in which the utopian element can emerge if people realize what their powers are. Such hopeful images can also be found in the country fair and circus where the anticipatory illumination is embedded in what Bloch terms *Wunschland* (the land of wishes). The dazzling side shows with exotic scenes and characters at the fair, and the magical performances of trapeze artists and tightrope walkers set the imagination free to envision change and sense the aroma of the earthly paradise. The routine of everyday life has no place at the fair and circus, nor does it have any place in westerns, adventure stories, and detective novels. An avid reader of Karl May, Kipling, Stevenson, Verne, and comic strips, Bloch argued that popular literature carried forth the anticipatory illumination of courtly romances and fairy tales. "The captivating fairy tale is therefore the adventure story; it continues to live today as colportage. . . . The dream of colportage is: never again everyday life; and in the end there is happiness, love, victory" (1974a:88).

1 *Messianism and Utopia.*

Throughout Bloch's commentaries dealing with fantasy literature and popular culture, anticipatory illumination is both seductive and disruptive. The reader/viewer is to be carried away and to undergo a sensation of estrangement (*Verfremdung*) while reading detective stories, adventure novels, westerns, and fairy tales or while watching plays and films. This estrangement allows the reader/viewer to glean the *Novum* because customary time and place are broken down, allowing for a different sense of perception. Although the reader/viewer is productive in his or her own right, the anticipatory illumination must also be a product of an artistic or a social sensibility that seeks to anticipate the way toward the classless society. If the *Vor-Schein* anticipates the classless society, it also awakens a sense in the reader/viewer about how fragmentary and unfinished the world is in order to urge its completion. The aesthetic truth of the *Vor-Schein* depends on the manner in which the artistic composition draws upon concrete correlates in the world and projects the possible realization of utopia. Here the idealistic and symbolic allure of the anticipatory illumination is substantiated by its critical-material position vis-à-vis intransigent social conditions:

> Consequently utopian function must essentially prove its worth along the same line against the ideal as it does against utopias themselves—along the line of concrete mediation with material ideal-tendency in the world, as mentioned. In no way can the ideal be taught and rectified through mere facts. On the contrary, an essential part of the ideal is that it has a strained relationship to mere established fact. On the other hand, the idealistic, if it has any worth, has a connection to the process of the world, of which the so-called facts are reified-fixed abstractions. The idealistic has in its anticipations, if they are concrete, a correlate in the contents of hope of tendency-latency. This correlate makes possible *ethical ideals as models, aesthetic ideals as anticipatory illumination, which point to the possibility of becoming real.* Such ideals rectified and conveyed through the utopian function are altogether those of a humanly-adequate expounded content of the self and the world. (1974a:296)

Here we can see the connection to Bloch's concept of Messianism as ethical model and his notion of anticipatory illumination. In his reading of the Bible, Bloch refers to Moses and Jesus as *Stifter* (instigators) of religions who carry a message of hope as messianic figures, illuminating through their actions how people can uncover the divine light in themselves through their acts and behavior—their struggle toward an upright gait (*aufrechter Gang*). Significantly, Bloch chooses the German word *Stifter* in his discussion of Moses and Jesus as ethical models who carry with them anticipatory illumination. The word *Stifter* is generally translated into English as founder, but Bloch could have used the more traditional German word *Gründer*, if he had wished. Instead, he chose *Stifter*, I believe, to describe Moses and Jesus because the verb *stiften* has a double meaning: (a) to found or establish; (b) to cause or stir up. It is because of the double meaning that I am using the word instigator, for Bloch saw Moses and Jesus not only as founders of religions but causing trouble, stirring up people to move—move against and away from the despotic rulers who were deluding and exploiting them in the direction of a *paradise on earth*.

Bloch did not believe that religion was to be *grounded* (*gegründet*) or fixed in any way. Religion was a part of a process of human hope that can only be kept alive through Messianism.[6] This is why Bloch argued the following:

> messianism in religion is the utopia which enables the Utterly Different of religious content to be mediated in a form in which it contains no danger of lords' anointment and theocracy: as Canaan in unexplored splendour, as the wonderful (miraculous). Judaism became rigid in the armour of the cult laws but messianic faith was kept alive through all codified epigonism; it was misery, it was above all the promise in Moses and in the prophets, irrefutable by any empiricism, which kept it alive. 'Whoever denies messianism denies the whole Torah,' says Maimonides; and it is the greatest Jewish teacher of the laws who says this, a rationalist and no mystic. The glad tidings of the Old Testament run against Pharoah and sharpen on this antithesis their lasting utopia of deliverance. That which is meant by Pharoah, Egypt and the kingdom of Edom is just as much the negative pole of Moses' glad tidings as Canaan is its positive pole. Without Egypt there would be neither exodus nor such evidence of messianism; but if Egypt is engulfed in the sea, the path to the holy dwelling becomes clear—there the Apocalypse, too, is latent in Moses. (1986:1241)

Bloch insists that the historical origins of Moses and Jesus are important because they point to a distinct time when humankind began to stand up and realize what course it had to take to create a paradise on earth. The scriptural records are intended to show something "utterly different" through the miraculous signs in the lives of Moses and Jesus that set them apart from all other saviors, leaders, founders, and gods. That is, the fantastic occurrences in their lives and the miracles that they performed constitute the anticipatory illumination as a messianic sign, and the messianic impulse within the anticipatory illumination, its religious and ethical nature, creates the criteria, in my opinion, for distinguishing between true fantasy and *Kitsch*.

To understand the messianic nature of Moses and Jesus is to understand the revolutionary nature of their historical advent, and why they distinguished themselves, *founders as instigators*, from other founders of religions by celebrating the divine in humankind. Bloch defines the role of religious founders:

> A founder is of course everywhere, but he becomes very clearly manifest only where he sets his new god against traditional customs, against natural religion empty of men; above all where he and his followers cling fanatically to him. It was thus that Moses and Jesus first emerged, were believed in as saviours, not just as mythical teachers, not just as pointers towards salvation. Although the name of Orpheus, and also the names of natural-mythic orderer-founders, right up to the cosmomorphic Confucius, even Zoroaster, the messiah of astral light, are mentioned together with the gods, they nonetheless remain behind them, relate externally to them. The Dionysian founder *turns to froth* before his nature god, the astral-mythic founder *fades* before him, and even Buddha, the great self-redemption, *sinks at the end* into the acosmos of nirvana. *Moses, on the other hand, forces his god to go with him, makes him into the exodus-light of his people; Jesus pervades the transcendent as a human tribune, utopianizes it into the kingdom.* (1986:1191)

Ironically, the instigators of religion bring a light with them that will extinguish the traditional religious belief in a transcendent god or an otherworldly god. The miracles and mysteries in the Bible are indicative of the divine potential of humans to realize god in themselves and in their communal life with one another. Moses and Jesus as instigators provide the miraculous clues and signs, crucial for true fantasy literature, that point to this ultimate revelation. Not only are Moses and Jesus representative of all that is utterly different, but all that they say and do is intended to astonish and enlighten us—provoke us to become children of the light, following in their light, which is the light of anticipatory illumination.

In this regard, the qualitative dimension of fantasy literature can only be appreciated if we grasp the religious dimension of its messianic power in the anticipatory illumination that sheds light on the mystery and purpose of our existence. For Bloch (1986:1195-96), the telos of life is to be found in the miraculous (*das Wunderbare*), totally bound to the "utterly different" signs which appear in the Bible as a whole:

> And this remains decisive: *the Utterly Different also holds good for the ultimate humane projections from religion*. It is only the Utterly Different which gives to everything that has been longed for in the deification of man the appropriate dimension of depth. . . . The miraculous as the Utterly Different with regard to the objective religious world is here clearly the *most characteristic mysterium of joy*, triumphing in the religious hope-content of man, i.e. that which explodes itself into the Utterly Different.

The fantastic projection of religious hope in the Bible lays the foundation, according to Bloch, for the formation of secular hope that demands a reverence for the utterly different as good and sets ethical and moral markers to lead us to our final destination of home. It is in this sense that the Bible is the seminal book of all true fantasy literature. It is crucial for determining the essential connection between wishful longings for communication with the Divine and fantastic utopian projections of home that are rooted in humankind. Bloch elaborates:

> Certainly the wishful image in all religions, and even more powerfully in those of the messianic invocation of homeland, is that of feeling at home in existence, but one which does not see existence as confined to its clearly surveyable and so to speak local patriotic ranks of purpose. So that religion, *in its constant final relation to the last leap and the utopian Totum*, amounts to more than ethicizing and blander rationalizations, amounts to more than morality and clear surveyability even in Confucius, its strongest ethicizer. The wishful content of religion remains that of feeling at home in the *mystery* of existence, a mystery mediated with man and well-disposed to his deepest wish, even to the repose of wishes. *And the further the subject with his founders of religion penetrates into the object-mysterium of a God conceived as the supreme Outside or the supreme Above and overpowers it, the more powerfully man in his earth-heaven or heaven-earth is charged with reverence for depth and infinity.* The growing humanization of religion is not paralleled by any reduction in its sense of awe, on the contrary: the Humanum now gains the mysterium of something divine, something definable, gains it as the future creation of the kingdom, but of the right kingdom. (1986:1196-97)

When Bloch refers to the "right kingdom," "good," and "goodness," he associates it with truth. However, "the *truth* of teleology never consists of purposes already existing in finished form, but rather of those which are only just forming in the active process, always arising anew within it and enriching themselves" (1986:1374). The importance of art is to reveal the process through which we materially try to attain truth and thus to estimate what is humanely and objectively appropriate to our wishes for home, also known as

> happiness, freedom, non-alienation, Golden Age, Land of Milk and Honey, the Eternally-Female, the trumpet signal in Fidelio and the Christ-likeness of the Day of Resurrection which follows it: these are so many witnesses and images of such differing value, but all are set up around that which speaks for itself by remaining silent. The direction towards this materiality and not only logically enlightening entity must be invariant; this is discernible at every place where hope opens up its Absolute and attempts to read it. There is no doubt at all, and no doubt was left about it; an unilluminated, undirected hope can easily merely lead astray, for the true horizon does not extend beyond the *knowledge of realities*, but precisely this knowledge, when instead it is Marxist and not mechanistic, shows *reality itself as one of—the horizon* and informed hope as one commensurate with this reality. The goal as a whole is and remains still concealed, the Absolute of the will and of hope still unfound, in the agent of existing the light of its Whatness, of its essence,

of its intended fundamental content itself has not yet dawned, and yet the nunc stans of the driving moment, of the striving filled with its content stands ahead, utopian and clear. (1986:1375)

By grounding the essence of truth in the relationship between mystery and Marxism, Bloch fulfills part of his project in *The Principle of Hope* of providing a religious basis to Marxism and uncovering atheism in Christianity. This dual and paradoxical purpose has great ramifications for both philosophy and theology that are still being debated in discussions of liberation theology. What is of significance here, however, is the religious aspect of his aesthetic category of anticipatory illumination in *The Principle of Hope* and its implications for fantasy literature. As we have seen, Bloch's reading of the Bible, which cannot be separated from his critique of religion, depends on his interpreting the fantastic projections of the utterly different, the miraculous, as messianic signs that indicate the truth of what we are as humans and how we can arrive at the place (home) that we wish for, a home objectively commensurate with reality and our potential. Since we have never reached home nor have become truly enlightened—that is, since we have never really become "children of the light"—we must still find our way out of the darkness that is life, and we need art (and philosophy, too) to help show us the way by means of *Vor-Schein*. The difficulty is that much of art is mere *Schein*, as much of fantasy literature is, and this *Schein* deludes us into thinking that we can gain the final destination by conforming to certain prescribed notions of what a human being is, by reaching a consensus that is determined in advance.

In contrast, Bloch insists that we must conserve messianic and biblical notions of the utterly different within us, if we are to determine the truth of the direction that reality has taken. Fantasy literature that pacifies us, brings us in tune with reality, conceives utopias as harmonious reconciliation with the status quo, is pernicious and false. In fact, the truth of all fantasy literature can be judged by comparing its conceptualized motifs and vision with the *Vor-Schein* in the Bible. If fantasy does not instigate discontent and set us to thinking about how we can move beyond ourselves to realize traces and signs of hope that are connected to the humanization of nature and the naturalization of humankind, then it is banal. It is not fantasy in the true sense which is embodied in a religious sensibility, a reverence for the divine potential in humankind.

5. *Conclusion.*

There are, of course, many criticisms one could voice about Bloch's reading of the Bible. It is too idealistic. It neglects the patriarchal nature of messianism and the sexist—and in some cases, racist—signs in the Bible that feminist critics have analyzed in elucidating ways.[7] It is an ideological reading of the Bible that comes close to making Marxism into a spiritual if not mystical philosophy. Finally, it does not take into account differences in voice and narrative strategies within the Bible.[8]

Nevertheless, Bloch's reading of the Bible opens the text up to those approaches and questions he may seem to neglect. He does not deny them. After all, Bloch reads the Bible in the name of oppressed groups, for the other, with the intention to overcome racism, sexism, and discrimination. In the specific case of fantasy literature, a reading of Bloch reading the Bible forces us to confront important ideological questions and value judgments concerned with fantasy literature that are rarely discussed. Why do we have such a religious reverence for some works of fantasy and not for others? Why do some works of fantasy nurture our imagination and bring about self-awareness while much of fantasy deludes us and reconciles us to the status quo? Why do certain ethical and moral impulses become indelible in the Bible and how are they transposed in secular fantasy as the anticipatory illumination that plays upon our deepest hopes for salvation? How does fantasy literature act to subvert hypostatized notions of reality by providing something utterly different from approved normative expectations? Paradoxically, Bloch's secularization of the Bible demands that we pay tribute to the profound religious nature of fantasy literature, which, to be "good" and "true," must be messianic and disruptive.

What is also crucial for understanding Bloch's reading of the Bible is his *insistence* that we as readers ground our hope by becoming detectives. There is a mystery to be solved in the Bible. It is a mystery that cannot be solved. But if we learn to read the Bible according to Bloch's detective reading of the messianic signs, we may be able to read all fantasy literature that has appeared since, and all that is to come, by becoming children of the light. We will demand the same apocalyptic light from fantasy that we have traditionally demanded primarily from the Bible.

NOTES

Unless otherwise indicated, all translations in the text are my own.

1. Cf. Colin Manlove's "The Bible in Fantasy" and Mara E. Donaldson's "Prophetic and Apocalyptic Eschatology in Ursula Le Guin's *The Farthest Shore* and *Tehanu*" in this issue of *Semeia*.

2. Literally, Bloch's term *Menschensohn* means "son of human beings" or "son of humankind." Wherever possible I try to use humankind or humans instead of the more traditional and male-biased "man." Jesus is traditionally referred to as the "son of man," and this term is used by some of the scholars I quote. I have not changed their terms, but I have tried to offer alternate concepts and categories that, for me, make more sense today.

3. Although many critics have translated *Vor-Schein* as pre-appearance, I believe that this translation does not adequately address the notions of anticipation and enlightenment which are crucial for understanding what Bloch intended by creating this category. I have addressed this point in my introduction to Bloch (1988:xxxiii): "The utopian quality of a work of art is determined by its *Vor-Schein* or anticipatory illumination. The anticipatory illumination is an image, a constellation, a configuration closely tied to the concrete utopias that are lit up on the frontal margins of reality and illuminate the possibilities for rearranging social and political relations so that they engender *Heimat*, Bloch's word for the home that we have all sensed but have never experienced or known."

4. Kasper Hauser was born on September 29, 1812 in southern Germany. Taken from his mother about the age of three, he was placed in solitary confinement for unknown reasons until May 26, 1828, when he was found wandering about the streets of Nuremberg. He appeared to be a child of nature, a blank slate, and had to learn to speak and be "civilized" again. Five years later he was killed by an unknown assailant. Nobody ever learned the "true" story of Hauser's origins, nor had he been able to adapt to society once he returned to civilization. The case of Kasper Hauser is well-known in Germany and has captured the imagination of such German writers as Jacob Wassermann and Peter Handke and the German filmmaker Werner Herzog.

5. Bloch uses the term *Novum* to designate the startling and unpredictable new that is always at the forefront of human experience and indicates the qualitative reutilization of cultural heritage. The *Novum* in works of art never dies. It is through the *Novum* that we orient ourselves and reshape the inconstruable question about the nature of human existence in concrete ways, in the materiality of culture, so that we can see more clearly the direction of utopia linked to messianism.

6. Cf. Bloch's remarks in *The Principle of Hope* (1986:1193): "And if the maxim that where hope is, religion is, is true, then Christianity, with its powerful starting point and its rich history of heresy, operates as if an essential nature of religion had finally come forth here. Namely that of being *not static, apologetic myth, but humane-eschatological explosively posited messianism*. It is only here—stripped of illusion, god-hypostases, taboo of the masters—that the *only inherited substratum capable of significance in religion lives: that of being hope in totality*, explosive hope."

7. Cf. Mieke Bal, 1986 and 1990, and Tina Pippin, "The Heroine and the Whore: Fantasy and the Female in the Apocalypse of John" in this issue of *Semeia*.

8. Cf. Robert Alter, 1990 and 1992.

Works Consulted

Alter, Robert.
- 1990 "Sodom as Nexus: The Web of Design in Biblical Narrative." Pp. 146-60 in *The Book and the Text: The Bible and Literary Theory*. Ed. Regina M. Schwartz. Oxford: Basil Blackwell.
- 1992 *The World of Biblical Literature*. New York: Basic Books.

Bal, Mieke.
- 1986 "The Bible as Literature: A Critical Escape." *Diacritics* 16:71-79.
- 1990 "Dealing/With/Women: Daughters in the Book of Judges." Pp. 16-39 in *The Book and the Text: The Bible and Literary Theory*. Ed. Regina M. Schwartz. Oxford: Basil Blackwell.

Bloch, Ernst.
- 1974a *Ästhetik des Vor-Scheins*. Vol. 1. Ed. Gert Ueding. Frankfurt am Main: Suhrkamp.
- 1974b *Ästhetik des Vor-Scheins*. Vol. 2. Ed. Gert Ueding. Frankfurt am Main: Suhrkamp.
- 1977a *Atheismus im Christentum: Zur Religion des Exodus und des Reichs*. Vol. 14 of *Gesamtausgabe*. Frankfurt am Main: Suhrkamp.
- 1977b *Experimentum Mundi*. Vol. 15 of *Gesamtausgabe*. Frankfurt am Main: Suhrkamp.
- 1986 *The Principle of Hope*. 3 vols. Trans. Neville Plaice, Stephen Plaice, and Paul Knight. Cambridge: MIT Press.
- 1988 *The Utopian Function of Art and Literature*. Trans. Jack Zipes and Frank Mecklenburg. Cambridge: MIT Press.

Hudson, Wayne.
- 1982 *The Marxist Philosophy of Ernst Bloch*. New York: St. Martin's.

Schwartz, Regina M., ed.
- 1990 *The Book and the Text: The Bible and Literary Theory*. Oxford: Basil Blackwell.

PROTOTYPIC HORROR:
THE GENRE OF THE BOOK OF JOB

Roger C. Schlobin
Purdue University—North Central

ABSTRACT

The book of Job presents readers with numerous difficulties; horror theory may resolve many of these. In its profound presentation of the problem of evil, its refusal and inversion of conventional signifying systems, and its monstrous representation of God, Job qualifies as one of the greatest works of horror. The book of Job distorts the readers' images of the natural order and reverses the reader's expectations (of justice, of a moral order), much as contemporary horror literature and films do. Like them, Job presents the readers with an anti-wisdom which takes perverse comfort in the triumph of evil over decency. By the end of the book, the righteous man Job has been devastated by God; what he has gained is at best the revelation that God is capricious, cruel, and always beyond human understanding.

---

1. Introduction: Job's Genre.

In responding to David Pellauer's 1981 essay "Reading Ricoeur Reading Job," Alan W. Olson articulates the dilemma of the book of Job's genre that has long troubled biblical scholars:

> In the matter of Job's silence we are driven to the brink of the void, if not directly into it, for the meaning of reference is eclipsed and annihilated. We are confronted, it would seem, by a genre of literature that goes beyond the tragic.... (116)

By not proceeding and identifying the genre "beyond the tragic," Olson reflects an old bafflement with the book of Job's literary type. In 1959 Norman K. Gottwald observed that it is "... a work so unique that it does not fall into any of the literary genres of antiquity or modernity" (472), and in 1979 W. Lee Humphreys added it eludes strict classification (202). Indeed, Joseph Campbell's 1949 edict that "categories ... are totally shattered by the Almighty of the Book of Job, and remained shattered to the last" (148, see also Penchansky:23) seems to have remained the governing assumption in any search for the work's literary identity.

However, the critical perspectives of the fantastic may be able to identify the nature of the book of Job. Like the Greek tragedy to which it is often compared and like the dystopian, it is an example of the larger mode or genre of horror. In fact, comparing the characteristics of the book of Job to those established for more modern works reveals it as a prototype of horror and horror's inexplicable and uncontrollable agony.

The three, critical elements of horror are: (1) its distortion of cosmology (more specifically, in Job's case, theodicy); (2) its dark inversion of signs, symbols, processes, and expectations that causes this aberrant world; and (3) its monster-victim relationship with its archetypal devastation of individual will (for a full discussion of these key elements of horror literature, see Schlobin *passim*). Most of these elements have been identified by biblical scholars as existing in the book of Job; so a portion of what will be done here is to assemble their insightful pieces of the puzzle.

2. *Distorted Cosmology.*

In all of horror's refractions, the aberrant world or distorted cosmology is one of its required characteristics. H. P. Lovecraft offers one of the best descriptions of this environment: it is "a certain atmosphere of breathless and unexplainable dread" within which there is "a malign and particular suspension or defeat" of those "safeguards against the assault of chaos . . ." (15). In a more general literary context, Northrop Frye's final stage of irony, the demonic epiphany, echoes this environment:

> The dark tower and prison of endless pain, the city of dreadful night in the desert, or, with a more erudite irony, the *tour abolie*, the goal of the quest that isn't there, [a] blasted world of repulsiveness and idiocy, a world without pity and without hope . . . . (1957:239)

Beyond either of these descriptions, horror's world must initially begin as a normal one, just as the book of Job does with Job's favored state. Yahweh, himself, in his early conversation with the Accusing Angel, offers testimony of Job's quality and the proper rewards he has received:

> God said [to the Accusing Angel], "Did you notice my servant Job? There is no one on earth [sic] like him: a man of perfect integrity, who fears God and does nothing wrong."
> The Accuser said, "Doesn't Job have good reason for being so good? . . . You bless whatever he does . . ." (Mitchell, 1987:6)[1]

In addition to the presence of a normal world and even as order crumbles to chaos, there must be the futile hopes of success, triumph, and/or escape. For example, Job demonstrates such optimism by his "sporadic moments of hopefulness and intimations of vindication" (Greenberg:292), consternation, and cries for justice. A number of scholars recently have reinforced this point: Edwin Good observes that Yahweh's speeches "taunt Job's lack of power and invite him to exert power he doesn't have" (369); Bruce Zuckerman suggests that the Poet of Job creates a "vision of renewal and resurrection so that he can ultimately and utterly discredit it" (134). Thus, as with the later Gothic setting, the characters with whom readers identify or empathize have nowhere to go; they are trapped within the incomprehensible.

Here the observations of biblical scholars serve them well. Paul Ricoeur (whose *The Symbolism of Evil* was the subject of a 1981 issue of *Semeia*, edited by John Dominic Crossan) observed that the book of Job is "... an upsetting document that records the shattering of the moral vision of the world" (314) and has a cosmology within which humanity hardly exists (78). Loretta Dornisch agrees that, in Job 38, order is beyond human knowing (epistemology) (6). André Lacocque adds that there is no real, accurate retribution in the world (36), that God demonstrates "that there is no ethical dimension in the natural realm, only in the societal" (45), and that God's response to Job and Job's subsequent submission are "unexpected and properly incomprehensible" (34). Joseph Campbell reinforces such visions by his statement that God makes no attempt to explain any of the distortions (1949:147), such as the wager or the lack of justice. As Good suggests further, "The God plays arbitrary, unmotivated games with 'peoples' (vv. 23-24) in 'lightless dark'" (255). Job knows that his world and expectations have been inverted. Early in the poem, in reaction to Bildad the Shuhite's criticism of his complaints, Job says:

> He [Yahweh] does not care; so I say
>   he murders both the pure and the wicked.
> When the plague brings sudden death,
>   he laughs at the anguish of the innocent.
> He hands the earth [sic] to the wicked
>   and blindfolds its judges' eyes.
>   Who does it, if not he? (Mitchell, 1987:28)

Later, in his response to Zophar the Namathite, he further laments his suddenly discordant world:

> Why do the wicked prosper
>   and live to a ripe old age?
> Their children stand beside them;
>   their grandchildren sit on their laps.
> Their houses are safe from danger,
>   secure from the wrath of God.
> Not one of their bulls is impotent;
>   not one of their cows miscarries.
> Their grandchildren run out to play,
>   skipping about like lambs,
> singing to drum and lyre,
>   dancing to the sound of the flute.

They end their lives in prosperity
  and go to the grave in peace. (Mitchell, 1987:52)

3. *Inverted Signs.*

The second major element of horror is that evil, cosmic inversion is at its heart. Considering the book of Job's ongoing fascination, it's not surprising it shares this characteristic with other enduring works of literature, like Shakespeare's *Macbeth* and *Othello*, Milton's *Paradise Lost*, and Dante's *Divine Comedy* among just a few. Job identifies one of the major elements of inversion when he tells Bildad the Shuhite of the reversal of friendship and love:

> All my friends have forgotten me;
>   my neighbors have thrown me away.
> My relatives look through me
>   as though I didn't exist.
> My servants refuse to hear me;
>   they shun me like a leper.
> My breath sickens my wife;
>   my stench disgusts my brothers.
> Even young children fear me;
>   when they see me, they run away.
> My dearest friends despise me;
>   I have lost everyone I love. (Mitchell, 1987:48-49)

To clarify this further, Ricoeur is off the point of Job's complaints and anguish when he remarks, generally, that "... etiological myths testify that man's most moving experience, *that of being lost as a sinner* [my stress], communicates with the need to understand and excites attention by its very character as a scandal" (3). The reason, of course, that this applies only peripherally is one of the many major inversions in the book of Job: Job isn't a sinner although he is punished and treated as one. A more pertinent observation than Ricoeur's is that the great works of literature transfix by the fascination of evil and by their characters' attempts to unravel and uselessly rationalize its machinations prior to any attempts at explanation. Certainly, neither Job's friends nor Yahweh present him any clarification, direction, or explanation.

Horror's and the book of Job's distortions of their normal worlds are based on violation of all expectations, such as Yahweh's of his covenant with Job (Mitchell, 1987:6, 8, 73). Alan W. Olson (in the quotation that opened this paper) captured this perfectly when he said that "the meaning of reference is eclipsed and annihilated" (116) in the book of Job. Moshe Greenberg, in *The Literary Guide to the Bible*, adds that "reversal and subversion prevail throughout" (283). Penchansky adds intention and suggests that the Job poet "writes out of a sense of pain, of dislocation, a feeling of wrongness . . . " (20), and Edwin Good says that the light of Genesis has been turned into darkness in Job's case (29, 191, 196-97, 204-5).

This concept of the corruption of meaning has drawn the attention of scholars of the horrific. Rosemary Jackson, in a discussion of what she calls the "uncanny," says horror "empties the 'real' of its 'meaning'" and removes the significance from signs (68). Jackson is, in part, right: the real is emptied, and modern illustrations, which also strip assumed meanings from what is perceived as "real," are such films as *Invasion of the Body Snatchers* (1956; novel by Jack Finney as *The Body Snatchers*) and *The Stepford Wives* (1975 from Ira Levin's novel). James B. Twitchell draws conclusions similar to Jackson's, postulating that horror ". . . is the art of generating breakdown, where signifier and signified can no longer be kept separate . . ." (1985:16). From the biblical side, Dornisch adds that "Job 38 is a magnificent example of religious language which climactically presents the *extraordinary in the ordinary* and thereby *reorients by disorientation*" (14). Richard Jacobson, in "Satanic Semiotics, Jobian Jurisprudence," detects a similar pattern of destruction or inversion of meaning by pointing out that the book of Job's "relentless contradiction . . . signifies relentless alienation, a primary uncertainty, an essential paradox" (63). Then, when it tries to "*achieve conviction*" (65), I would add that nothing results; all of Job's efforts are fruitless. Justice is never delivered; piety yields torment; social approval becomes public degradation; ". . . images of death constantly put the cap on the images of life" (Good:272; see also Zuckerman:118-35).

Most importantly (and what Jackson, Twitchell, Dornisch, and Jacobson do not mention), horror, generally, and the book of Job, specifically, substitute new meanings for signs. Rather than stripping significance from signs, horror fills them with inverted and deadly meanings, repugnant to the victims and attractive to the monsters (or to those who relish horror's punishment of its victims [Ebert:*passim*; Schlobin:39-45]). Job senses this early in the poem:

> Why is there light for the wretched,
>   life for the bitter-hearted,
> who long for death, who seek it
>   as if it were buried treasure,
> who smile when they reach the graveyard
>   and laugh as their pit is dug.
> For God has hidden my way
>   and put hedges across my path.
> I sit and gnaw on my grief;
>   my groans pour out like water.

> My worst fears have happened;
>   my nightmares have come to life.
> Silence and peace have abandoned me,
>   and anguish camps in my heart. (Mitchell, 1987:14)

Since meaning has fallen, Job has no chance to understand his punishment. Thus, horror's and the book of Job's relations between sign and meaning will not yield to the coercion of any human's reason, experience, wisdom, intelligence, and most of all, individual will. As Stephen King has described, terror "arises from a pervasive sense of disestablishment, that things are in the *unmaking* [my stress]" (22). I would further expand this to say that the "unmaking" is followed by an unnatural and unholy *making* that no one, reader or character, can understand or coerce.

Specifically, what are the natures of other distortions in the book of Job? The most obvious is the inversion of Job's relationship with Yahweh, which changes from covenant to betrayal, the "cosmic breach of faith" (Sewall:11) sometimes typical of the tragic. Unbeknownst to Job until halfway through the poem ("... God has tricked me,/ and lured me into a trap" [Mitchell, 1987:48]), his relationship with the divine is subjugated to a wager of which he is the subject. Affirming such betrayal, André Lacocque points out that the book of Job is about the impotence of religion and philosophy (42), and within the frame of inversion, religion becomes nihilism and existentialism (for want of a less modern term) and philosophy becomes idiocy.

Once this context is understood, inversions fall from the book of Job like the proverbial manna. Other scholars have indicated that there is something wrong with the law of retribution (Crenshaw:101, Dornisch:5), and Paul Ricoeur has gone so far as to say the book of Job renounces it (322). Clearly, Job's suffering is undeserved (Crenshaw:101, Dornisch:5); it is pointless torture. The unjustified pain—the death of his sons and daughters, the horrible skin disorder, the poisoned breath (Mitchell, 1987:7, 8, 21, 23, 49)—occurs because sin, the proper cause of retribution, is absent from horror or the book of Job since sin, to exist at all, presumes a standard of absolute morality. In a cosmos completely ruled by chance and wager, divine torment is the game and good is irrelevant; evil masquerading as good stands alone, unchallenged and supreme. There is no moral order in the book of Job. It follows, then, that justice is not to be found in the natural order of things, since it too assumes good (Curtis:498, citing Tsevat:73-106). Job's legal pleading must become no more than babble, and Bruce Zuckerman speculates that the poet of Job saw his protagonist as the "ultimate fool" (47). Job summons only Yahweh's unresponsive presence, and while Northrop Frye may see only "something irrational in divine providence" (1990:108), the text indicates that

Yahweh's dominance is fully irrational (see the discussion of Yahweh as monster and the element of justice below—especially Lacocque's and Ricoeur's observations—for further elaboration).

Of course, another, extensive illustration of distortion and inversion is Job's friends' reactions. Biblical scholar William Morrow accurately indicates that the wisdom theology spouted by Job's friends can be dismissed as a falsification of reality (221, also citing Tsevat:91-92); Lacocque concurs that their arguments "amount to a pious lie" (35; also see Greenberg:302-3 below); and Good identifies Bildad's reasoning as circular (218). Charles Muenchow's "Dust and Dirt in Job 42:6" provides wise insight into why Job's friends' support and nurturing turn into demeaning criticism. Muenchow chronicles the competitive place honor has as a social phenomenon directly related to power and authority (600). According to Muenchow, the friends see an opportunity to humiliate, diminish, and demean Job (608-609). Shame (601) and the reduction of his power and social position result, both serving two functions here. One, Job's friends are constant reminders of the contrast between the assumed world order, which is no longer functional, and Yahweh's new stance. Two, they anticipate contemporary, gloating, and safe audiences who also vicariously enjoy seeing virtuous victims punished by monsters; friendly comfort, for Job, is nonexistent and ineffectual (Good:232, Zuckerman:101).

4. *God as the Monster.*

Often, in the modern horror film, audiences view this punishment through the monster's eyes (Ebert:*passim*) and see the victim begging them for the mercy that is never given. Frequently, these victims, like Job, are the admirable, the successful, the justifiably proud, and the advantaged. Sadly, there is significant evidence that horror's audiences, and Job's friends, gloat over the agonies of the privileged (for a survey of the scholarly comments and an analysis of audiences enjoying victims' suffering, see Schlobin:39-45). One of the most stinging analyses of modern American audiences' responses to suffering is offered by John Fraser in *Violence in the Arts*:

> ... the legions of blue-collar American readers of scandal tabloids and crime magazines obviously enjoy being assured of the omnipresence of violence, cynicism, and corruption, since it makes their own decently undramatic lives appear more admirable in contrast. (115)

While it may be intellectually and historically invalid to compare Job's friends to Fraser's "blue-collar Americans," it is nonetheless not too far a leap to see smugness and relish in the friends' attacks on Job as they ironically believe they know the truth and use it to promote themselves socially at Job's expense without any efforts of their own. Further, it is tempting to think of the book of Job's Yahweh as the anthropomorphic creation of the "friends" or, at least, as someone like them who existed in the author's mind.

Ultimately, what the inversions of signs and processes in the book of Job show is how the horrible wager destroys moral processes and perceptions. Thus, the inversion is the history of how Job's piety, which once brought him regard and favor, now yields extreme punishment (for a discussion of how Eliphaz's "pernicious arguments undermine piety," see Greenberg:291). At the end, and as André Lacocque has observed, "In anguish, we [and Job] discover the total collapse of meaning" (46). Nor is there any real promise that the future will be any better since hope has been transformed into dread. Early in the poem, Job's response to Eliphaz the Temanite indicates that "all hope has been driven away" and later adds "like a cloud my hope is gone" (Mitchell, 1987:21, 71). If there were any doubt, Yahweh affirms this at the end of the poem from the whirlwind: ". . . hope is a lie" (Mitchell, 1987:86). This is made darker by the complete absence of any mention of an afterlife anywhere in the poem and strong indications that physical death is final (Mitchell, 1987: 36-37). Thus, there is no benevolent promise that Job's suffering in this life will be rewarded in another.

Yahweh, along with horror's monsters, is in accord with Lacocque's "collapse of meaning" and some biblical scholars' descriptions. In general, horror's creatures are blatantly oblivious to any human senses of order, ethics, or morality. They are so evil that good is either unknown or has no impact on them (just as Yahweh is more interested in the wager than in Job). Their natures are incomprehensible to the epistemologies of their victims (see Mitchell, 1979:100), and monsters are completely capable of disintegrating their victims' bodies and souls. Job reveals this knowledge about his own monster when he responds to Eliphaz the Temanite:

> But he wills, and who can stop him?
>   What he wishes to do, he does.
> He will go ahead with his plans,
>   devising my endless torment.
> This is why terror grips me;
>   when I think of it, I am appalled.
> He has wrung the strength from my mind
>   and pumped my heart full of sorrow.
>   (Mitchell, 1987:59-60)

Thus, in the standard manner of horror, Yahweh renders Job's will and spirit impotent.

In most modern horror, monsters can come in any form, both natural and supernatural, and frequently they mirror the dark sides of their creators. However, those who have examined Yahweh have taken an extreme view and have paralleled Leslie Fiedler's identification of horror's monster as alien: ". . . the abominable, to be truly effective, must be literally unspeakable" (121). Lacocque says that the nature of creation in the book of Job, unlike the standard in much of the Old Testament, is the work of an impersonal deity who lacks ethical standards; he points to the deity of Israel's scriptures, for whom "justice" is not a trait (38), as the governing power in the book of Job. In the same vein, Frye indicates that "One can understand, up to a point, the Gnostic inference that the God of the Old Testament was an evil being; one remembers that most mythologies have a trickster god . . ." (1990:107). Ricoeur is less historical but far more emphatic. For him, Yahweh is a destructive enemy (54), and ". . . the violated [inverted] pact makes God the Wholly Other and man nothing in the presence of the Lord" (50, 81; see also Mitchell, 1987:viii; Good:241; Zuckerman:46). As extreme as Ricoeur is, his view may be most accurate. From the inception of the wager through Yahweh's challenging words (Curtis:497), Job is helpless before the irrational forces and punishments forced upon him. Yahweh is a divine solipsist who has no expectation of losing the wager or suffering any consequences.

And it is Job's helplessness that reflects the usual "relationship" between monster and victim in horror. As scapegoat and victim, Job must be open to the monster's invasion, from his most basic level of intimacy to his obvious social status. The monster, Yahweh here, is the omnipotent master, and he shatters Job's ". . . protective hedge bit by bit" (Crenshaw: 102) with his "brute power" (Good:375). Job is stripped of even the most basic defenses and assurances he expects from either civilization or the divine.

As Yahweh's victim (Lacocque:39; Mitchell, 1987:vii), Job is typical of most in horror and reflects its simplest element: he offers admirable familiarity to his audience. He is undeniably virtuous (Greenberg:286) and pious, being neither dupe nor dolt. The book of Job opens with his praise (Mitchell, 1987:5). He knows he is innocent (Lacocque:35; Campbell, 1949:147; Mitchell, 1987:viii) despite his punishments and his friends' unrelenting insistence to the contrary. He is brave and resolute, showing not the slightest indication that he "recants or in remorse grovels before the divine" (Curtis:505).

His "undeserved suffering" and justified responses (Crenshaw:101, Dornisch:5) are also quite common among the horror that has followed the book of Job. This is where Joseph Campbell appears to identify Job incorrectly. Although Campbell glorifies him and parallels him to

Prometheus, Christ, Atlas, and Loki (1968:415), these figures had at least some justification for their pains and, most significantly, had control over their choices and actions, which Job simply does not. All suffer for far more than a wager as do the protagonists of the Greek tragedy that has been equated with the book of Job. No, Job is not a member of this group. He has not transgressed against the gods. He has none of the characteristics of the tragic hero: he lacks freedom (Sewall:45), control, and defects (fatal flaw, *hamartia*, or *hubris*). Rather, he is pointlessly "terrorized" (Mitchell, 1987:x), humiliated, debased, and forced to inescapably endure wretched suffering (Morrow:221; Mitchell, 1987:viii; Penchansky: 79). He tries to depend on his knowledge, his wisdom, his will, but all are devastated by divine oppression. As in most horror, the devastation is made more agonizing because Job knows it is happening but is incapable of understanding or preventing anything: he suffers but is unaware of the necessity or reasons for a "'boundary-situation' not of his own making" (Sewall:46).

A critical key to the magnitude of Job's debasement is the widely cited line involving "dust" or "dust and ashes." It has been translated in a variety of ways and has been the subject of much debate among biblical scholars. Stephen Mitchell provides "comforted that I am dust" (1987:88). Morrow cites a multitude of translations that include "consoled for dust and ashes," "I reject dust and ashes," "I consider myself dust and ashes," "I am become dust and ashes," "I reject and forswear dust and ashes" (212-213, 221), and a possible synthesis "I retract (*or* I submit) and I repent on (*or* on account of) dust and ashes" (211). Muenchow suggests further that Job sinks to or is sitting on dust and ashes (609). The obvious consistency here, about which there appears to be little debate, is the recurrence of "dust and ashes." This may be the answer of Job's fate and the key to what has happened to him. The breath of God has been sucked from him. As a result of this, and according to Moshe Greenberg, Job has assumed "qualities of insubstantiality (4:19), lifeless malleability (10:9), worthlessness (13:12) . . ." (302-3). Job has been reduced to a pre-creation state, de-evolved and returned to nothing more than the clay of the Earth (Good:228, 307, 340; see also Mitchell, 1987:xiii), less than human. Job foreshadows this in one of his answers to Bildad the Shuhite, ". . . you [Yahweh] formed me from clay/ and will soon turn me back to dust" (Mitchell, 1987:30) and identifies himself with "dust" on, at least, four other occasions (Mitchell, 1987:24, 30, 45, 72). Most cruelly, he does not become insentient "dust"; his consciousness and awareness of his wretched state remain when the divine is withdrawn from him.

5. *The Quest for Wisdom (and Its Failure).*

There have been those who have spoken of a final reward for Job. Joseph Campbell thinks he gains terrible wisdom as the result of his suffering (1968:415). Paul Ricoeur (quoted by Dornisch:5) calls Job's plight tragic and speaks of restoration. Both of these scholars assume Job's experience has meaning, but it does not. By definition, his knowledge is not wisdom; it lacks the necessary component of understanding to be wisdom. All that the defenseless Job knows is omnipotent fact and whimsy, both imposed without explanation and without any attempt to provide accompanying comprehension. Thus, while his being lacks the creative breath of God, Job's environment, his cosmos, can be perceived as an anti-Eden. In Genesis, the blissful Adam and Eve, with their pre-lapsarian innocence, had facts without understanding. The tortured Job, trapped within the irony of his divinely-created Hell-on-Earth (the inversion of Eden), also has fact (his suffering) and also lacks understanding. However, his world, unlike Adam and Eve's sanctuary, is oppressive and deadly. All three characters have factual knowledge; none have comprehension (with the possible exception of Adam's naming of the creatures); one, Job, suffers amid a divine inversion that maims the nature of all knowledge and makes wisdom irrelevant, if not a mockery, for humanity. He points directly to this when he says to Zophar the Namathite:

> Doesn't the mind understand
>   as simply as the tongue tastes?
> Do all men grow in knowledge?
>   Are they wise because they are old?
> Only God is wise;
>   knowledge is his alone. (Mitchell, 1987:33)

Moreover, when Job's suffering ceases, he is only provided with revelation (Sewall:46) and alleviation, not reward and understanding, and there is little indication in the text that all is returned to him. His dead, for example, are not revived (Good:189, 388-89). What remains to him is the irrevocable truth that all can be taken from him again at any time regardless of his piety, faith, or social standing—what Stephen Mitchell calls "a ferocious hymn of de-creation" in his analysis of the end of the poem (1987:xiii). Such ultimate deprivation of security, love, and trust is a common characteristic of horror at its most revulsive. There are no happy endings. The monsters can always come again (witness the current multitude of film sequels). Characters may survive, as Job does, but they do so as savaged beings who have paid vast emotional and psychological prices (like Northrop Frye's *desdichado*, figures of misery or madness [1957:238-

39]). At its very best, and as Dornisch (7) and Ricoeur have suggested, the book of Job *might* have taught him and others "how to suffer suffering."[2]

If this jigsaw puzzle of observations, "horrific scholarship," and biblical scholarship does work, how is it that it has remained incomplete for so long? Have the assumptions that the book of Job is in some way didactic or wise distorted the ability to recognize its true nature? It would appear that the common assumption that the book of Job is among the examples of "wisdom literature" has forced people well away from the text itself. An examination of Norman K. Gottwald's cogent and representative definition of such literature might confirm this:

> If we . . . think of wisdom *as a nonrevelatory mode of thought that focuses on individual consciousness of truth and right conduct, displaying a humanistic orientation and a didactic drive* to pass on its understanding to others, it is easy to see "wisdom" almost everywhere in the Hebrew Bible where there is no direct speech of God. (1985:567)

However, it is not "easy to see" the book of Job within this description. What Job learns of truth is obviously revelatory: it is the "direct speech of God" and certainly does not require any rational "mode of thought" from him or his friends (see Mitchell, 1987:34; Good:234-35). The Yahweh of the whirlwind might just as well be stating the law of gravity without explanation for all the understanding that is offered or found. No, Yahweh's "truth" is only bare fact; it does not contain or require wisdom or understanding. Moreover, if the "wisdom" of the book of Job were not even for Job, but for readers, what might be the didactic messages? "Do not be too pious, for you will draw the Accuser to you"? "At all costs remain unnoticed; then, you can even be evil"? "Be the second-most virtuous person in the world and you will not suffer"? "Knowledge and wisdom are for gods, not humans"? If anything, the moral is that there is no certainty from the divine. Everything can be taken away and maimed for nothing more than a wager.

A second possibility for what seems to be the missed discovery of the poem's obvious horror revolves around the issue of text. Anyone who has ever done any research on the book of Job knows that the poem is encrusted with exegesis and commentary. These are fascinating studies in themselves but too often hide the poem from scholars rather than reveal it. I would suggest that the centuries of commentary are the source of the view of the book of Job as "wisdom through suffering," not the text itself. Thus, it has been taught, and so it has been learned, and so it has been taught in a recurring cycle within which the book of Job itself may have been lost or obscured.

Yet a third possibility may be that the poem's awesome range and power take it so far beyond the limits of traditional academic disciplines that it requires an approach as wide-ranging and interdisciplinary as the fantastic to begin to capture it. And it could very well be unreasonable to expect anyone in a single discipline to engage the book of Job. Also, David Penchansky may be partially correct that, for many, the poem is filled with "... disharmonic elements that resist aggressive interpretation" (19). Further, it may be that biblical scholars may either intelligently refuse to subject themselves to the horror genre, or, perhaps, they consider it sub-literary?

6. *Conclusion.*

With or without these three possibilities, the book of Job has drawn unceasing attention. It would seem from all the comments by biblical scholars and others that its astonishing, archetypal misery may, in itself, be its appeal, that the need and attempts to rationalize it with the assumption of a just universe may, itself, be the compulsion that has enthralled so many minds. This agonizing and baffling fascination with the nature of the book of Job and its evil (as well as its horrific successors and their unavoidable, evil natures) among thoughtful scholars and readers and, perhaps, the author of the book of Job may be explained by Leslie Fiedler when he says, in *Love and Death in the American Novel*, that "evil is real and . . . the thinking man breaks his heart trying to solve its [evil's] compatibility with the existence of a good God or his own glimmering perceptions of Goodness" (418).

Within this heartbreak and throughout the millennia, the book of Job's heinous poison has festered beneath poultices of exegesis. Often, the venom is unrecognizable beneath adhesive rationality and intellectual evasion. If the poem is, indeed, as horrific as portrayed here, then any rational approach that assumes order and benevolence is certain to slap layers of insulation and disguise over it. Job's story may be the most soul-chilling work of all time; no wonder so many have placed intellectual balms on its piercing darkness. Moreover, its deadly fangs have been all the greater since it is set within accompanying literature that lulls unsuspecting readers into false expectations of comfort and healing. Minds have justifiably quailed before the book of Job and fearfully hidden it beneath the machinations of interpretation. The human has recoiled from the non-human, from the void, seeking escape from the truly hideous Other that violates all sanctuaries and sensibilities. Few other works are so unexpectedly nihilistic; few others have offered such potent and persistent infection.

NOTES

1. Stephen Mitchell's revised 1987 translation of the book of Job, used exclusively here, does not use chapter and verse. Thus, references to the text are page numbers.

2. Dornisch is citing and quoting Ricoeur's "Toward a Hermeneutic of the Idea of Revelation," *Harvard Theological Review* 70 (1977): 12.

WORKS CONSULTED

Campbell, Joseph
    1949   *The Hero with a Thousand Faces*. A Meridian Book. Cleveland: World.
    1976   *The Masks of God: Creative Mythology*. New York: Penguin.

Crenshaw, James L.
    1981   *Old Testament Wisdom: An Introduction*. Atlanta: John Knox.

Curtis, John Briggs.
    1979   "On Job's Response to Yahweh." *Journal of Biblical Literature* 98:497-511.

Dornisch, Loretta.
    1981   "The Book of Job and Ricoeur's Hermeneutics." *Semeia* 19:3-21.

Ebert, Roger.
    1981   "Why Movie Audiences Aren't Safe Anymore." *American Film* 6:54-6.

Fiedler, Leslie A.
    1960   *Love and Death in the American Novel*. New York: Criteron.

Fraser, John.
    1974   *Violence in the Arts*. Cambridge: Cambridge University Press.

Frye, Northrop.
    1957   *Anatomy of Criticism: Four Essays*. Princeton: Princeton University Press.
    1990   *Words with Power: Being a Second Study of "The Bible and Literature"*. San Diego: Harcourt Brace Jovanovich.

Good, Edwin.
    1990   *In Turns of Tempest: A Reading of the Book of Job with a Translation*. Stanford: Stanford University Press.

Gottwald, Norman K.
    1959   *A Light to the Nations: An Introduction to the Old Testament*. New York: Harper.
    1985   *The Hebrew Bible: A Socio-Literary Introduction*. Philadelphia: Fortress.

Greenberg, Moshe.
    1987   "Job." Pp. 283-304 in *The Literary Guide to the Bible*. Ed. Robert Alter and Frank Kermode. Cambridge: Harvard University Press.

Humphreys, W. Lee.
  1979   *Crisis and Story: Introduction to the Old Testament.* Palo Alto: Mayfield.

Jacobson, Richard.
  1981   "Satanic Semiotics, Jobian Jurisprudence." *Semeia* 19:63-71.

Jackson, Rosemary.
  1981   *Fantasy: The Literature of Subversion.* London: Methuen.

King, Stephen.
  1981   *Danse Macabre.* New York: Everest.

Lacocque, André.
  1981   "Job or the Impotence of Religion and Philosophy." *Semeia* 19:33-52.

Lovecraft, H. P.
  1945   *Supernatural Horror in Literature.* New York: Abramson. Reprint. New York: Dover, 1973.

Mitchell, Stephen, trans.
  1979   *Into the Whirlwind: A Translation of the Book of Job.* Garden City: Doubleday.
  1987   *The Book of Job.* San Francisco: North Point.

Morrow, William.
  1986   "Consolation, Rejection, and Repentence in Job 42:6." *Journal of Biblical Literature* 105:211-25.

Muenchow, Charles.
  1989   "Dust and Dirt in Job 42:6." *Journal of Biblical Literature* 108:597-611.

Olson, Alan M.
  1981   "The Silence of Job as the Key to the Text." *Semeia* 19:113-19.

Penchansky, David.
  1990   *The Betrayal of God: Ideological Conflict in Job.* Louisville: Westminster/John Knox.

Pellauer, David.
  1981   "Reading Ricoeur Reading Job." *Semeia* 19:73-83.

Ricoeur, Paul.
  1967   *The Symbolism of Evil.* Trans. Emerson Buchanan. Religious Perspectives 17. New York: Harper & Row.

Schlobin, Roger C.
  1988   "Children of a Darker God: A Taxonomy of Deep Horror Fiction and Film and Their Mass Appeals." *Journal of the Fantastic in the Arts* 1:25-50.

Sewall, Richard B.
  1959   *Vision of Tragedy.* New Haven: Yale University Press.

Tsevat, M.
  1966   "The Meaning of the Book of Job." *Hebrew Union College Annual* 37:73-106.

Twitchell, James B.
   1985   *Dreadful Pleasures: An Anatomy of Modern Horror*. New York: Oxford University Press.

Zuckerman, Bruce.
   1991   *Job the Silent: A Study in Historical Counterpoint*. New York: Oxford University Press.

BIBLICAL NARRATIVE AND CATEGORIES OF THE FANTASTIC

Peter D. Miscall
St. Thomas Seminary

ABSTRACT

The narrative of the ten plagues and the event at the sea in Exodus 1-15 is an interesting test case for reading biblical narrative as a type of fantastic literature. The narrative is a fascinating mix of divine and human elements. The plagues and crossing of the sea are obviously miracles, yet the characters, especially Moses and the Israelites, are very human in their actions and responses. Great marvels of weal or woe have little lasting effect on humans, but telling the story, the fantasy, of those marvels can cause joy and trust in God. Loss of the joy and wonder of fantasy leaves Israel only with the harsh realities of history.

---

1. Introduction: Retrospective.

I approach the topic of the Bible and Fantasy from the perspective of a student of the Hebrew Bible, especially the narrative corpus in Genesis-2 Kings. Lately my work has included concern with Isaiah, his imagistic universe and his relation to the book of Genesis. About two decades ago when I first became disenchanted with the disintegrative methods of historical-criticism, I, like many other biblical scholars at the time, turned to literary criticism for an alternative vision and encountered French Structuralism. In some biblical circles, the names of French literary critics such as Barthes, Todorov and Greimas began to replace those of American and German biblical critics such as Albright, Cross, Noth, and von Rad. Structuralism had its heyday in the 1970s with effects that linger till the present time. However, in the course of the 1970s and the 1980s, it gave way to a wide variety of literary critical methodologies and the names of the above French critics all but disappeared from the pages of biblical criticism.

I think that structuralism formed an apt bridge from historical-critical approaches to the open-ended poststructuralism of today. Structuralism, on the one hand, moved away from the atomistic strategies that divided and sub-divided the biblical texts into sources and their diverse parts and from the assumption that meaning lies in reference to an extra-textual historical reality. On the other hand, it still, as historical-criticism did, offered a "science of literature"; structuralism, not historical-criticism, would provide the meaning, the one interpretation, of a biblical text. Today, the biblical scholarship which comes after structuralism finds itself in a pluralistic situation that no longer speaks of a "science of biblical criticism" or the one true interpretation. It is a scholarship that can produce a collection of essays on the Bible and Fantasy.

Let me return to the early 1970s when I and others were seeking a bold new way to finally reveal the meaning of biblical literature. Many of Tzvetan Todorov's works, which sought a grammar or poetics of literature, were influential, and Robert Scholes's *Structuralism in Literature* was a major guide to the entire field. At the time I also read Todorov's *The Fantastic*, a study of mainly 19th century fantastic tales, and Scholes's *Structural Fabulation*, a study of 20th century science fiction and fantasy. (I also note Cixous's study of Freud's *The Uncanny* which provided insight into this adventurous mode of writing and reading.) This was fascinating for me, but since it did not seem to have any direct relevance to my work on biblical narrative, I did not pursue it. The books and articles remained on my shelves unread and unconsulted for 15 or more years.

When asked to submit an article to this volume, I responded positively mainly so that I could pursue a new area of study. I assumed that fantasy meant fairy tales, such as those of the brothers Grimm and as studied by Jack Zipes. I was pleasantly surprised to see Todorov's *The Fantastic* listed along with works by Jack Zipes and Rosemary Jackson, and I find myself turning more to it, to Scholes's *Structural Fabulation*, and to several of Aichele's articles for this essay than to the work of Zipes and Jackson. I have also had the benefit of reading, at least in draft if not final form, most of the articles in this volume.

Whether it is science fiction, fantasy such as that by Tolkien or LeGuin, or fairy tales, particularly their modern retelling, fantastic literature helps us see our ways, our life, and our world differently and, we hope, better. This effect can be on any part of that world, including its literature. For example, science fiction, usually placed in the future and frequently in another world, can lead us to envision new possibilities and dangers in our present situation and can also turn us back to reconsider how we represent, how we talk about and portray that world, whether in a technical, scientific language or in literature, particularly narrative fiction. Science fiction and other fantasy literature highlights, in its own powerful fashion, what we can do (and cannot do) with language: its strengths and its weaknesses, its potential and its traps.

One of the traps is the assumption of realism, the belief that a narrative can capture and perfectly mirror reality. Even if fictional in terms of characters and events, a realistic narrative is still about human life as it is really lived. "Traditionally, realists have claimed a close and direct correspondence between their models and the world around them" (Scholes, 1975:6). Fiction is *poiesis*. "Fiction" is Latin based, "poiesis," Greek based; both words refer primarily to something being made and constructed. For Scholes (1975:7), "All writing, all composition, is construction. We do not imitate the world, we construct versions of it. There is no mimesis, only poiesis. No recording. Only constructing."

Aichele (1989:42-46) briefly discusses the role of literary fantasy in exposing the illusion. Citing Rabkin's work, he notes that what is fantastic in literature at one time can later become normal and expected; a new work of fantasy, then, questions this normality. Fantastic literature operates with major literary innovations which upset the generic conventions and draw attention to them as conventions, as literary devices. The Russian Formalists developed a similar point with their notion of *defamiliarization*, the process by which a literary work makes aspects of reality, including other literary works, look strange and new to us; literature makes the familiar new and in some ways unrecognizable.[1]

This connects with Scholes's more general point "that fiction is about other fiction" (1975:1). Any literary work, fantastic or realistic, exists in relation to other works. Our understanding of one work is affected by our knowledge of these others and our reading of the latter, in turn, is affected by our reading of the one given work. These "other works" can be expanded to include critical writing about literature. In a standard view, criticism is about literature and is therefore a totally separate genre of writing. Literature is creative and original; criticism is secondary and parasitic. Much biblical commentary is based on this view. In a newer view, whose proponents would claim reflects much critical practice from the inception of literary criticism, the separation is not so radical or distinct. Criticism has its own creative impulses; it is a conversation partner with literature and not a mere neutral observer. Literary writers are affected by critics just as much as the latter by the former. Indeed, great poets are frequently great critics, such as Wordsworth, Coleridge, and Eliot. I bring this somewhat lengthy discussion to a close with the image of a literary world peopled with writers, both literary and critical, and their works, all existing in a complicated network of relations. This is not a closed or finished network; literature may always be striving for the closure of system, but another work, literary or critical, is always to be written and added to that world. And that added work can recast and change that world.

2. The Hebrew Bible and The Fantastic.

In this essay, I look at the Hebrew Bible, mainly at the first part of Exodus, as part of this literary universe. If a literary work can serve to defamiliarize our views and notions of reality and of other literature, then criticism can serve to defamiliarize our views and ways of reading given literary works, especially works that are comfortable because we know how to read them.[2] I propose to use categories and insights from the study of fantasy to look anew at Moses, Pharaoh, God and the plagues; I do not propose to use a particular definition of the fantastic, whether Todorov's or another's, as a set genre to interpret a biblical text. My essay concerns the Bible and Fantasy, not the Bible as Fantasy.[3]

Todorov locates the fantastic between two other genres. In the uncanny, "the laws of reality remain intact and permit an explanation of the phenomena described," while in the marvelous "new laws of nature must be entertained to account for the phenomena" (41). In the fantastic, there is a profound hesitation between these two explanations. Faced with an inexplicable event, character(s) and reader remain uncertain as to whether the event is reality or dream, natural phenomenon or supernatural miracle. I want to use the categories of the uncanny and the marvelous in more inclusive ways than Todorov does and to separate them, at most stages of the reading, from the notion of hesitation and uncertainty.

In the French, the uncanny is *l'étrange* which also means the strange, the curious, and the unusual. I think that these are more appropriate terms for much of the biblical narrative that I discuss. For example, faced with the burning bush, Moses's response is more one of curiosity than of awe before the uncanny. "Let me turn aside to see this wonderful sight, why the bush is not burned" (Exod 3:3). The marvelous includes the miraculous, the superhuman, and the supernatural which, in antique literature, are closely allied with the mythic. I look at my chosen biblical texts with these expanded categories of the fantastic and with the idea of the hesitation in the background.

3. The Exodus.

The miraculous and the supernatural occur at points throughout the narrative in Genesis-2 Kings; these are the places where an event or an outcome are explicitly ascribed to divine intervention. God did it! I focus on the major miracles of the Hebrew Bible, that is, the signs and wonders of Exodus, the ten plagues and the event at the sea.

Exodus opens with the note that the Israelites are fulfilling the divine commands of creation by being fruitful and filling the land (Exod 1:7; Gen 1:28). The allusion to creation casts a mythic overlay on the following narrative of the Exodus. This overlay continues in the themes of lethal threat and wondrous, if not divine, deliverance in the first two chapters. Moses's birth story marks him as an exceptional man, a man of destiny; this is a fine example of Josipovici's fairy tale beginning (83-85; 193-200). God's notice, at the close of the second chapter, of the threats to his people is immediately followed by his call and commissioning of Moses in the burning bush episode. The narrative in Exodus 1-6 leading up to the plagues is clearly in the realm of the marvelous and the miraculous: God acts and speaks and Moses is given signs (Hebrew: ôt).[4]

The issue in chapter 4 is the people's trust and belief and their willingness to listen and act on what they hear. The two Hebrew verbs, āmēn (to trust) and šāma (to listen, obey), both contain ideas of willingness to act on what is believed or heard. Moses is given the signs of the rod, the leprous hand, and blood turned to water because he is afraid that the people "will not believe me or listen to me but will say, 'The Lord did not appear to you'" (4:1). The need to persuade the people is connected with acts that will be seen. In their first encounter with the people, Moses and Aaron gather the people, tell them of the Lord's desire to deliver them and perform the signs

> in the sight of the people. They believed, and when they heard that the Lord had taken note of his people and their suffering, they bowed and they worshipped. (4:31)

The intended result is achieved, at least for a while.

There is nothing wondrous about the narrative of increased oppression in Exodus 5. Moses and Aaron make their demand of Pharaoh but perform no signs. Pharaoh, understandably, asks "Who is the Lord that I should listen to him?" To this point the wondrous acts are connected with trusting, hearing, and acting on what is heard and believed. The Israelites, faced with the increased work demands, rebuke Moses and Aaron and seriously question their leadership. No signs, no trust.

In a typical pattern for the narratives in Exodus and Numbers, the people complain to Moses (and Aaron), Moses appeals to the Lord, and the Lord responds.

> Now you will see what I will do to Pharaoh. With a mighty hand he will set them free; with a mighty hand he will drive them from his land . . . Moses told this to the Israelites but they would not listen to Moses because of their crushed spirit and their harsh labor. (6:1, 9)

Moses sees and speaks, but the Israelites do not listen.

4. *The Plagues: Divine Wonders.*

Exodus 7:1-6 introduces the narrative of the plagues as a clash between divine power and Pharaonic power; however, this is not a match of equals since the Lord is the only contender with power. Pharaoh and the Egyptians are passive and acted upon. The narrative of the plagues and the event at the sea in Exodus 7-15 is, in some ways, the Israelite version of the myth of creation as a conflict between the creator god and forces of chaos, frequently in the form of a sea monster or dragon.5 Genesis 1-2 presents creation as God's unilateral acts without any resistance from any other source; God speaks and acts and the world comes into being (Levenson:53-77). The narrative in Exodus 7-15, in contrast, is suffused with themes and imagery of power, "signs and wonders," and destructive conflict; and it is the people Israel, not the world, that comes into being. On the other hand, the conflict, before it even starts, is over because all effective power lies with the Lord. "I will harden Pharaoh's heart . . . and he will not listen to you" (7:3-4). In this parody of myth, the antagonist of the Lord ultimately derives his power from the Lord. In the last five plagues, including the death of the firstborn, Pharaoh and the Egyptians refuse to be convinced by the Lord's mighty hand and by his signs and wonders because the Lord hardens their heart (9:12; 10:1, 20, 27; 11:10; 14:4, 8, 17). God sets up his own enemy. As Northrop Frye notes, the Bible, in simple but powerful fashion, addresses and defuses ancient myths by turning them into literary images and themes (92). The Bible, in effect, defamiliarizes the myths of ancient Canaan, Mesopotamia, and Egypt.

The plagues and the hardened heart transpire so that the Lord can multiply his signs and wonders, show his power and might, and be glorified in the midst of Egyptian and Israelite (7:3; 9:16; 10:1-2; 14:4, 17-18) who will all come to know "that I am the Lord" (7:5; 10:2; 14:4, 18). Pharaoh and the Egyptian army are finally destroyed in the waters of the sea.

> Israel saw the great act [Hebrew: wondrous hand] that the Lord performed against the Egyptians; the people stood in awe of the Lord, and they trusted the Lord and Moses his servant. (14:31)

Miracles and wonders, performed with power and might, are seen, and this leads to awe, trust, and knowledge. The plagues and the event at the sea are the main divine signs and wonders of the Hebrew Bible; there is no doubt or hesitation that these are the mighty acts of the Lord. They belong in Todorov's category of the marvelous and are overlaid with mythic themes of creation, creation conflict and the predestined savior.

5. *The Plagues: Human Response.*

This is only part of the story, a synopsis of the Exodus events such as found in Psalms 77, 78, 105 and 114. The actual narrative in Exodus 1-15 contains many human and natural aspects that offset and modify the miraculous and divine. Although Moses is the predestined savior from birth, he is fully human, and not superhuman. God acts through him and Aaron and the rod; Moses does not possess any magical or wondrous powers in his own right. His objections to the divine call almost block the predestined course of events and perhaps usher in the frightening attempt by the Lord to kill him (4:24-26). The initial signs and reports by Aaron and Moses convince the people only for a short while; for the Israelites a harsh turn of events cancels the effect of miraculous signs.

The Egyptian magicians are a different qualifying element. Their rods also turn to serpents, but Aaron's swallows theirs (7:8-13). When Moses turns all the water in Egypt into blood, "the magicians of Egypt did the same with their spells, and Pharaoh's heart was hardened" (7:22). However, a more powerful demonstration would have been to turn the blood back into water; their magic only increases the plague. Pharaoh realizes this with the plague of frogs. "Frogs came up and covered the land of Egypt. The magicians did the same with their spells and brought frogs upon the land of Egypt" (8:6-7). This is ludicrous and a mockery of Egyptian power; even Pharaoh acknowledges it since this time he hardens his heart only after his pleas have caused the Lord to remove all the frogs (8:8-15). The magicians are unable to match the plague of gnats and recognize that this, and probably all the plagues, are the work of God (8:18-19). Finally, with the sixth plague, the magicians cannot appear before Moses for even they are afflicted with the personal humiliation of boils (9:11). There is a strong element of humor and ridicule here.

Perhaps the most striking aspect of these awesome signs and wonders is that they have little lasting effect on any of the characters involved. Pharaoh and the Egyptians may pause, but then they keep pursuing the Israelites even after the gruesome deaths of their firstborn. The event at the sea is not a wonder to convince them to turn back; it is a catastrophe in which they are annihilated. For the Egyptians the effect of miracles is short-lived; nothing, except their destruction, will cause them to let Israel go. The Israelites' trust and awe are also short-lived; the narratives of Exodus and Numbers are mainly about their complaints and rebellions. The wonders of Exodus turn quickly into the misery of wandering. The bitter waters at Marah are the first example (15:22-25). The people complain and ask what they will be able to drink; they do not ask Moses or the Lord to perform a wonder like those they have just witnessed.

As already noted, Moses (and Aaron) remain very human throughout.[6] Moses can be frustrated and resentful (17:1-7) and weak. He needs others to help him even if he does not realize it himself (17:11-12), and this help can come from the unexpected quarter of a foreigner, a Midianite priest (18:13-27). The awesome theophany and revelation at Sinai do not change this state of affairs as the episode of the Golden Calf in chapters 32-33 makes clear. The people lose heart and Moses, faced with this rebellious people, wants more divine signs to assure him that he is and will be a successful leader (33:12-33). God does not comply.

6. *Fantasy: Hearing and Trusting.*

The explicit divine interventions of Exodus fall in the realm of the marvelous, of fantasy; we are not dealing with a transcription of historical reality. Realism fails. The human elements, on the other hand, point to what Scholes calls "the failure of fantasy." No one has ever "succeeded in imagining a world free of connection to our experiential world . . . reality can neither be captured nor escaped" (1975:7-8). As miraculous as the events of Exodus 1-15 are, they are still connected to the world we live in; the marvelous and the realistic combine inextricably in this narrative.

In a slap at the Judeo-Christian tradition, Scholes speaks of a universe "subject to the capricious miracles of [the] deity" (82). This may hold for many parts of that tradition, but it does not hold for this biblical narrative of the archetypal miracles of the Exodus. In the seventh plague of thunder and hail, God first sends Moses to Pharaoh to proclaim that the point of these continued plagues is the knowledge that "there is no one like me in all the earth." God has let Pharaoh survive "to show my power and to recount my name through all the earth" (9:14-16).

The narrative of the tenth plague, the death of the firstborn, is broken at points by the proclamation that the feast of Passover is to be observed this night and then, as a memorial day, it is to be observed throughout the coming generations as a perpetual rule (12:14).[7] The proclamation, in the midst of a narrative of the past, prescribes what is in effect a narrative of a ritual observance that should occur annually and forever. The rite will be a memorial of God's mighty acts when God brought the people out of Egypt and, indeed, created them as Israel, the people of God.

> When your children say to you, "What does this rite mean to you?" you will say, "It is the Passover sacrifice to the Lord. He passed over the houses of the Israelites in Egypt when he struck the Egyptians and spared our houses." (12:26-27)

In response, "the people bowed and worshipped"; this is the identical response to Moses and Aaron's first report of the Lord's call and performance of the signs at the end of chapter 4. In this instance, the people need only hear; they see no signs or wonders.

The injunction to connect the Passover rite with the story of the Exodus is repeated twice in 13:8-9 and 13:14-16. The rite itself is now a sign (ôt) "so that the teaching [tôrâ] of the Lord may be on your lips" (13:9). The marvel of the sweetened waters at Marah, mentioned previously, is followed by the more mundane establishment of "a statute and an ordinance" and the proclamation that Israel will not be struck as the Egyptians were if they will listen to the Lord and pay heed to his commandments (15:25-26). Teaching, listening, observing, and doing are all human acts, not capricious miracles of the deity. As noted above, trusting and hearing both refer to the willingness to act on what or whom is trusted and heard.

Keeping Passover includes telling the Exodus story, the Exodus fantasy; interestingly, a significant part of that story is the injunction to observe Passover. Recounting this fantasy is to show the Lord's power and to recount (sippēr) his name so that all will know that there is no God like him (9:14-16). Other gods and their myths are mocked in disguised form; Pharaoh and his hardened heart stand for Baal, Marduk, and a host of other creator gods. The Egyptian magicians can only respond with a ludicrous and ultimately vain show of power. The Exodus tale is, at once, an impressive, instructive, and enjoyable story. In all the literary analysis, I do not want to lose sight of this most human aspect of story and fantasy; fantasy is entertaining, enjoyable, and inspiring on a multitude of levels. I can analyze many of the levels, but I cannot analyze the enjoyment and the inspiration without losing them.

> Moses recounted [sippēr] to his father-in-law all that the Lord had done to Pharaoh and the Egyptians for Israel's sake . . . and Jethro *rejoiced* for all the good the Lord had done for Israel when he delivered them from the Egyptians. Jethro said, "Blessed is the Lord . . . Now I know that the Lord is greater than all other gods." (18:8-11)

Jethro has only to hear of, not see, the Lord's mighty acts to praise them with joy. He is the first in a long line who hear of these signs and wonders and respond with joy. Awe, joy, trust, and knowledge should come from hearing and not just from seeing.

I am making a clear distinction between actual miracles that may or may not have occurred in history and the continued recounting of this story of miracles. It is the latter that I am concerned with. I am also claiming that the biblical narrative itself is making an analogous distinction. In the narrative, these great wonders in Egypt and at the sea accomplish little if anything in terms of persuading people to change their views and actions for a significant time. On the other hand, hearing or reading the narrative should lead to joy and trust in the Lord. The narrative of the revelation at Sinai continues this theme.

> The Lord said to Moses, "I am coming to you in a thick cloud so that the people will hear me speaking to you and will then trust you forever." (19:9)

In a previous article, I dealt with the narrative material in Exodus 19-24 and focused on the recurrent concern with hearing and trusting or believing, rather than with seeing and trusting. The people at Sinai, at the time of this great theophany, see and hear only thunder and lightning (19:16-18; 20:18-21). They do not see God or, with the possible exception of the Decalogue itself (20:1-17), hear his actual words to Moses. They hear Moses's reports of what the Lord said and respond positively (19:7-8; 24:3); surprisingly, Moses writes these words in the book of the covenant and immediately reads the book to the people who again respond positively (24:4-7). The people, in this instance, are like all later Israelites and like us; they hear through reading.

Any sense of trust in the Lord and the actions, the way of life, that follows from it are ultimately based on hearing and reading the word of God. Miracles may occur and be impressive, but they have little staying power. A story of miracles, a fantasy, is another matter entirely. Therefore, any hesitation or uncertainty concerning this biblical narrative is not so much about whether an event in the narrative is divine or human from the point of view of character(s) or reader as it is about the narrative as a whole from the point of view of a later reader or hearer. (Such hearers and readers are posited in the narrative itself in the children of the Israelites in Egypt and in Jethro.) Is this narrative a human story or the word of God? If the narrative has any impact on a reader, is this an effect of a good story or is it the work of God?

7. *They Did Not Live Happily Ever After.*

From a contemporary and Western view, the Exodus with its plagues and sea event are a variation of the motif of the cavalry riding to the rescue. The narrative is a good, rousing tale. This is De Mille's and Heston's interpretation in *The Ten Commandments* and in the screen version, which reflects a frequent understanding, the cavalry comes at the close of the story and "then they lived happily ever after" as in a fairy tale. In the Hebrew Bible, in contrast, the cavalry comes at the beginning of the story, and the fairy tale is followed by the intrusion of reality "in the form of real failure and death" (Josipovici:84). Just in Exodus 15:22-17:15, the Israelites encounter in order: bitter water, no food, no water, and a violent enemy, the Amalekites. Each intrusion of harsh reality is countered by a divine intervention; the marvelous and the supernatural offset the human and the natural.

However, this rapidly changes in the narratives of Exodus 32-34, Leviticus 10, and Numbers 10-36.[8] In Exodus 32, the Golden Calf episode, the Lord's wrath blazes and he wants to annihilate Israel as he annihilated Pharaoh and the Egyptian army. Moses may talk the Lord out of this extreme measure, but many Israelites die in the aftermath and the Lord strikes the people, not the Egyptians, with a plague (32:35).[9] Fantasy turns to Horror; Divine Hero turns to Divine Ogre (see Schlobin in this volume). The wrath that once fell upon the Egyptians to deliver the Israelites now falls upon the Israelites to threaten that very deliverance.

The fairy tale is interrupted by real failure and death. For the people who left Egypt, who were delivered from there amidst many signs and wonders and by the Lord's mighty arm, the story ends when their dead bodies fall in the wilderness (Numbers 14). They die outside the land and never realize the settlement and possession promised 40 years before (Exod 3:7-17; 15:13-17). Their children, led by Joshua, enter and settle in the land, but their story, and the stories of their descendants, are mainly tales of failure and death. The wondrous fantasy of the Exodus has apparently been lost; the loss is confirmed, in ironic fashion, in the narrative of a time of hope, the reign of Josiah.

> The king commanded all the people, "Keep the passover to the Lord your God as written in this book of the covenant." For this passover had not been kept since the days of the judges who judged Israel, all the days of the kings of Israel and Judah. But in the eighteenth year of king Josiah, this passover to the Lord was kept in Jerusalem. (2 Kgs 23:21-23)

As others have observed, Josiah's reform was mainly cultic and focused on proper worship and on worship centered in Jerusalem. In this report of Josiah's passover "in Jerusalem," there is no mention of anyone rejoicing in the marvelous tale of the plagues and the deliverance at the sea. Passover seems to be only a ritual observance, not a recounting of the Lord's mighty acts and of the Lord's name.

In this perspective, the events at Marah—the sweetened waters and the establishment of a statute and an ordinance (Exod 15:22-26)—combine fantasy and reality, miracle and everyday life. In this perspective, Israel's history through 2 Kings is a story of losing sight of fantasy and miracle and of reducing life to its harsh realities and trying to cope with them through rituals and statutes and ordinances. The Lord of Exodus with his outstretched hand and many signs gradually recedes from the people's view. The final chapter of the story, 2 Kings 25, mentions the Lord only in the designation, "the house of the Lord" (vv. 9, 13, 16); the length and detail of the chapter, including many Israelite and Babylonian proper names, emphasize the absence of God. The sweet waters of Marah which were for all Israel are replaced by Jehoiachin's daily meal in the presence of the Babylonian king (v. 29). Israel's story ends with a sorry tale of failure and death, an account far different from the fantasy with which it began so long ago.

NOTES

1. See Scholes (1974:74-91) for discussion and bibliography.

2. I speak of defamiliarization and making strange and not of subversion which is the chosen term of Jack Zipes and others for their studies of the fantastic, particularly fairy tales. I do this for the chosen focus and purposes of my essay and not to question or reject the fact that this defamiliarizing can also be powerfully subverting, especially when the work analyzed is considered to be the Word of God by so many.

3. Schlobin's essay on Job contained in this volume offers many valuable and original insights into Job by reading it through the lens of Horror, a particular category of the fantastic. He also argues that Job belongs solidly within the genre of Horror, that it is a work of Horror. This is the argument that I am not making with biblical narrative; I am not trying to fit the narratives into any one genre or literary category.

4. I use the words God and the Lord throughout my essay interchangeably because of my present concerns; I do not thereby imply that there is no distinction between *elohim* and *YHWH* in the biblical texts.

5. See Cross:112-44 and Levenson:3-50 for particulars and further discussion. In 4:1-5 Moses's magical rod turns into a snake *nahaš*; in Hebrew this is the normal term for snake. In 7:8-13 it turns into a *tannîn* which can also refer to the sea monster of creation as in Ps 74:13 and Isa 27:1, 51:9 (also note Gen 1:21). The great dragon, the Leviathan (Isa 27:1), is merely a rod that swallows other rods.

6. A more disturbing aspect of Moses's humanity is his relationship to and his treatment of his wife, Zipporah, and his two sons, Gershom and Eliezer. His meeting with and subsequent marriage to Zipporah are narrated in briefest form (2:15-22). Gershom's birth is reported in 2:22; Eliezer's existence is noted in 4:20, "sons," and his name given in 18:4. In 18:1-6, they are with Jethro when he comes to greet Moses and then drop from the narrative. Wife and sons play no role in Moses's continuing story. This may be due to his status as chosen and unique leader whose successor, Joshua, is designated by the Lord (Num 27:12-23); that is, he cannot pass his authority and power on to his sons (see Steinmetz), but it portrays him in (in)human light.

7. I do not enter into the complicated issue of the relation of Passover in 12:1-28 and 43-50 with the feast of Unleavened Bread in 13:3-10 and the consecration of the firstborn in 13:1-2 and 11-16. My focus is on the motivation for these observances and not on their relationships; therefore, I refer to them collectively as the Passover.

8. See Greenstein for an excellent discussion of the complications and ambiguities of the Nadab and Abihu story in Leviticus 10.

9. *Nāgap*, to strike with plague occurs in 7:27 and 12:23, 27 where it refers to a plague on the Egyptians; in 12:13, 23 it refers to the plague not afflicting the Israelites.

WORKS CONSULTED

Aichele, George, Jr.
    1989   "Literary Fantasy and the Composition of the Gospels." *Forum* 5:42-60.
    1991   "Literary Fantasy and Postmodern Theology." *JAAR* 59:323-37.

Cixous, Hélène
    1976   "Fiction and its Phantoms: A Reading of Freud's *Das Unheimliche* (The 'uncanny')." *New Literary History* 7:525-48.

Cross, Frank Moore, Jr.
    1973   *Canaanite Myth and Hebrew Epic: Essays in the History of the Religion of Israel.* Cambridge: Harvard University Press.

Freud, Sigmund
    1976   "The 'Uncanny.'" (1919). Trans. J. Strachey. *New Literary History* 7:619-45.

Frye, Northrop
    1982   *The Great Code: The Bible and Literature.* New York: Harcourt Brace Jovanovich.

Greenstein, Edward L.
    1989   "Deconstruction and Biblical Narrative." *Prooftexts* 9:43-71.

Josipovici, Gabriel
    1988   *The Book of God: A Response to the Bible.* New Haven: Yale University Press.

Levenson, Jon D.
    1988   *Creation and the Persistence of Evil: The Jewish Drama of Divine Omnipotence.* San Francisco: Harper & Row.

Miscall, Peter D.
    1987   "Hear and Believe Forever." *The Bible Today* 25:381-85.

Scholes, Robert
    1974   *Structuralism in Literature: An Introduction.* New Haven: Yale University Press.
    1975   *Structural Fabulation: An Essay on Fiction of the Future.* Notre Dame: University of Notre Dame Press.

Steinmetz, Devora
    1988   "A Portrait of Miriam in Rabbinic Midrash." *Prooftexts* 8:35-65.

Todorov, Tzvetan
    1973   *The Fantastic: A Structural Approach to a Literary Genre.* Trans. Richard Howard. Cleveland: Case Western Reserve University Press.

The Fantastic
in the Discourse of Jesus

George Aichele,
Adrian College

ABSTRACT

This paper explores selected longer dialogues and discourses of Jesus from the gospels, in terms of a theory of literary fantasy derived from the works of Tzvetan Todorov and Eric Rabkin, among others. A comparative approach is used, from which it may be argued that the earlier phases of the trajectory of the synoptic tradition tolerates the dimension of the fantastic in ways that later phases do not. The passages selected focus upon the identity of Jesus, his relation to the devil, and the relation of his words to the eschaton. In each case, the element of the fantastic is signaled by a greater degree of ambiguity or self-referentiality, which leaves undeterminable the genre and hence the truth-value of the text.

---

1. *Introduction.*

Tzvetan Todorov has defined the literary fantastic as interruptions of reference within a story which result in narrative hesitation or indeterminacy between the genres of the marvelous and of the uncanny. These are two distinct literary genres, representing two worlds or narratives of reality. The marvelous represents a supernatural world, a world in which the supernatural is really present and active, and the uncanny represents a world in which very strange events occur, but no matter how strange they are, they can be given a natural explanation. The theological differences between these two worlds are immense, and the fantastic hesitation between them corresponds to theological uncertainty.

The fantastic interruptions of reference render impossible the determination of identity—the identity of characters, of objects, of events, and ultimately of reality itself. The fantastic text is always a fictional text, and at these points of interruption it reveals its fictionality through a disruption of the screen of realistic representation. Fantasy turns literary realism—the illusion of reference to an extratextual reality—against itself, and it refers instead to its own fictionality—that is, to its own failure to refer. In this way, literary fantasy reveals the world of normal, everyday experience to be itself a fabrication, a necessary fiction made possible by the deceitfulness of language, and by the ontology which supports the illusions of realism.

I have argued elsewhere that the literary fantastic played a fundamental role in the composition of the canonical and non-canonical gospels, and that this element of the fantastic is to be found also in the smaller diegetic and mimetic units of which these larger texts are formed.[1] However, many generations have read the gospels as not at all fantastic, but rather as referring to historical or theological realities. On the basis of such readings, these readers have accepted or rejected the truth of these narratives. How is it that these millions of readers have been unable to detect the presence of the fantastic in the gospels?

Both believers and disbelievers have found the fantastic elements in the Jesus traditions to be unacceptable. Todorov argues that the fantastic requires "near belief," which is neither belief nor disbelief. Because of its generic ambiguity, the fantastic is inherently subversive of belief; fantasy resists even the "willing suspension of disbelief" essential to literary realism. It is unlikely that a community which wanted to believe —possibly undergoing persecutions from without or dissensions within— would willingly produce texts which made belief difficult. On the other hand, it is not unlikely that such a community might take received narratives which resisted belief and render them more readily believable—defantasize them. The fantastic element in the gospels has been obliterated and ignored in readers' efforts to make sense of the texts, to understand them as referring either correctly or incorrectly to reality.

2. *The Dialogues.*

In the canonical gospels, fantastic accounts of parables or miracles of Jesus are often juxtaposed with other accounts having similar content, or with allegorizing commentary by Jesus or others, or with non-fantastic narrative material (other sayings or deeds). This establishes a metatextual context within which the reader resolves the indeterminacy of meaning within these stories. These literary techniques distinguish the canonical gospels from writings such as the gospel of Thomas, where the absence of a significant context leaves the isolated sayings and brief dialogues of that collection quite enigmatic.

Likewise, the fantastic appears and disappears in the dialogues and longer discourses of Jesus, as they are represented in the gospels. An example of this may be found in Mark 7:14–23 and its parallels (Matt 15:10–20 and Gos. Thom. 14), in which a prominent role is played by the saying, "There is nothing which can go into a man from the outside and defile him; but it is what comes out of a man that defiles him" (Mark 7:15). Thomas's version of the saying comes at the end of a discourse by Jesus in which he apparently opposes fasting, prayer, and almsgiving, and advocates both healing the sick and eating "what [is . . .] set before you" (see also Luke 10:8–9a). In Mark and Matthew, the saying leads to questions from the disciples, followed by an explanation of the statement by Jesus.

In Thomas, there is no attempt to explain this saying in terms of the belly and the heart, as in Mark and Matthew, and it is not clear whether (good) healing is contrasted to that which defiles and "which issues from your mouth." Saying 14 conjoins several sayings which appear to be united only by their rejection of religious law and taboo. The mouth is an ambiguous place, where what goes in—apparently the food which the wandering healer is given—will not defile, but what comes out will defile. The mouth is the site of an enigmatic transformation; its function as boundary is disrupted and becomes paradoxical. The mouth is uncanny and yet also marvelous; this indeterminacy is an important characteristic of literary fantasy. It applies also to the remarks on fasting and praying, both of which involve the mouth.[2]

In contrast, the dialogue in Mark 7:18–23 provides a quasi-scientific explanation which weakens the fantastic reversal within the parabolic saying. However, the mouth (*to stoma*) does not appear in Mark's text, and that "which can go into [. . . and] comes out of a man" would not clearly refer to food, were it not for the larger narrative context of 7:1–8 and the narrator's commentary at 19b, one of Mark's asides to the reader. Also, although the paradoxical saying is presented before "the multitude," the clarifying remarks appear in one of several private conversations between Jesus and his disciples "away from the multitude" and therefore separating the disciples/insiders from the crowd/outsiders.

The attempt to clarify diminishes the element of the fantastic. Throughout Mark the reader, like the disciples and unlike the crowds, is privy to Jesus's secret instructions, including the allegorical de-fantasizing of the sower parable in Mark 4:14–20. Although its form is quite different, the de-fantasizing function of Mark 7:18–23 parallels that of the allegorizing of the sower parable. In addition, the grouping of parables around a common theme—the hidden made manifest, the small become great—provides a metatextual commentary for the parables of Mark 4. In contrast, Thomas's version of the sower parable (saying 9) has no commentary, and the seemingly random order of Thomas's sayings collection disrupts any metatextual effect.

However, the nature of Jesus's relation to the disciples and the crowds (as insiders and outsiders) is a continuing question in Mark, a question which Matthew eliminates.[3] Furthermore, the reader of Mark, like the disciples in Mark, lacks a necessary key to the interpretation of these sayings. The narrative is unable to explain itself, and it requires an external supplement. By the end of Mark, Jesus is no longer available to explain his words; neither the reader nor the disciples have yet seen the resurrected Jesus in Galilee (16:7). The tradition has attempted to resolve this by adding to the end of Mark. If these supplements are insufficient, then the reader must turn to other biblical texts (other gospels, epistles, the Hebrew scriptures) or to non-biblical authorities (creeds, commentaries, personal experience, etc.) in order to complete the text's meaning. Just as the scenes of private instruction make clear the disciples' stupidity, the asides to the reader in Mark make explicit the reader's stupidity; they are points at which the text announces its own artifice and demonstrates its own incompleteness. All of this adds to the greater uncertainty of the Markan explanation, in comparison to Matthew's version.

Matthew also presents the initial saying as a public one, but there is no indication that it is followed by a withdrawal of Jesus and the disciples from the multitude. In Matthew 15:17–20, the abridged reply of Jesus not only lacks both the narrative context of private instruction and the narrator's comment, but the "physiological" (uncanny) explanation removes the ambiguity of the saying, in contrast to Mark. The mouth is no longer fantastic; it is connected to the stomach, which excretes but does not defile, but also to the heart, which does defile a man.

Another example of the de-fantasizing of the fantastic in the discourse of Jesus may be found at Mark 3:22–27 par. Jesus reverses the words of scribes who charge that he is possessed by Beelzebub. Jesus's reply presents the paradox that if this is so, then "Satan rises up against himself" and "cannot stand."

> But no one can enter the house of the strong man and seize his goods, unless first he binds the strong man; then he can plunder his house.

This aphorism is closely paralleled by Thomas 35 (and less directly by saying 22), and it is more than a little reminiscent of Thomas 98 (the parable of the assassin).[4] Thomas 35 lacks Mark's preceding dialogue about the devil, and it has no evident supernatural reference. These sayings appear to have political and legal dimensions, with strong overtones of perhaps revolutionary violence which are often overlooked by exegetes seeking more "spiritual" interpretations.

As Mark 3:21–22 makes clear, part of the issue in this dialogue is who is to "possess" Jesus. In this episode, the crowd is apparently in the house with Jesus, and "his own people"[5] are outside, in contrast to Mark 7:17. However, the question of Jesus's alliance with Satan remains unsettled, for a paradox cannot decisively answer a question. Jeremias argued that the saying refers to the temptation of Jesus in the wilderness, following his baptism, but even if that is so, the Markan version of the temptation

(1:12–13) hardly clarifies the saying. The more detailed (and clearly marvelous) temptation stories of Matthew or Luke (from Q) may do so, although neither Jesus nor Satan "binds" the other in those stories. Thomas has no temptation account.

This passage also is followed shortly by another aside to the reader, "This was because they said he had an unclean spirit" (3:30), which apparently refers to vv. 28–29, about blasphemy against the Holy Spirit (*eis to pneuma to hagion*), and to v. 22, the accusation of the scribes. Once again, however, the narrator's comment conceals as much as it reveals. Does the statement of the scribes blaspheme against the Holy Spirit? Does the reader indeed know that Jesus's spirit is the Holy Spirit? Mark's depiction of the baptism of Jesus—when "the Spirit like a dove" descends upon him—is quite ambiguous, but Matthew and Luke make it explicit that the spirit which has come to Jesus at his baptism is the Holy Spirit (or Spirit of God).

Thomas 44 also includes a version of the saying about blasphemy against the Holy Spirit, but as is usual for Thomas, without any larger narrative context. However, Thomas's version of the saying, unlike Mark's,[6] clearly distinguishes between blasphemies against the Father or the Son, which will be forgiven, and blasphemy against the Spirit, which will not be forgiven "either on earth or in heaven."

The parallels to Mark's dialogue about Beelzebub appear in Matthew 12:22–30 and Luke 11:14–15, 17–23, which also include a large amount of material from Q. In these texts, Jesus's answer (to somewhat different audiences) is more forthright. In Matthew the sentence, "But if I drive out demons by the spirit of God, then the Kingdom of God has come to you," is inserted between the paradox and Matthew's version of the saying about the strong man. This provides a non-paradoxical alternative to the scribes' claim and reinforces the interpretations that the "strong man" is the devil and that Jesus's spirit is divine. The entire account is inserted into a longer, tightly organized story in which the good, miraculous powers of Jesus as the son of David are highlighted.

Luke removes Matthew's messianic allusions but also inserts a sentence between the paradox and the saying about the strong man; instead of the spirit of God, it is the finger of God by which Jesus casts out demons. "Spirit" is clearly a troublesome item in these stories! The saying has also been revised (Luke 11:21–22): instead of binding the strong man, the thief (who is "stronger") takes away "the armor in which he had trusted." Again the effect is to remove the indeterminacies which appear in Mark. It appears that the paradox had already been de-fantasized by the time that it was included in Matthew and Luke. There are important disagreements between Matthew's and Luke's versions of the dialogue, but in both cases, the search for a "spiritual" (marvelous or supernatural) interpretation has been augmented, and the possibilities of a "political" (uncanny but naturalistic) reading have been diminished.

This is at least in part a result of the juxtaposition of sayings in these writings; in a saying independent of any literary context, the paradox regarding Jesus's identity in Matthew 12:27-28 and Luke 11:19-20 would be no more decidable than the paradox of Satan divided in Mark 3:26. In the minimal context of the apparently random order of the gospel of Thomas, and without supplementary instruction, the reference of saying 35 is entirely indeterminate. Even in the far more contextually determined dialogue in Mark, Jesus's identity remains undecidable. In contrast, however, both Matthew and Luke stress that the kingdom has come "to/upon you" in the powerful actions of Jesus, and in case this is still unclear, the larger narrative contexts heavily reinforce this interpretation.[7]

3. *The Identity of Jesus.*

The determination of narrative reference depends in part upon how much the actual reader knows. For example, does the reader already know what is meant by Mark 1:1 when Jesus is described (in some manuscripts) as "the Son of God," or is the meaning of this phrase what the reader is trying to uncover?[8] If "son of God" is ambiguous, and especially if it cannot be determined whether this term refers to the uncanny or to the supernatural, then the fantastic dimension of the text of Mark becomes more apparent. Nor can Jesus simply be identified with "the son of man" in Mark. He is the son of man in the form of the one who refers to the son of man in the third person. Mark tells stories about Jesus, and Jesus tells stories about the son of man. This adds a further element of uncertainty to these passages.

Two dialogues in which this indeterminacy appears in Mark are the confession of Peter (8:27-30) and the interrogation of Jesus by Pilate (15:2-5). A striking contrast to Peter's confession is found in Thomas 13, where neither the simile offered by Peter (Jesus is "like a righteous angel") nor that of Matthew (Jesus is "like a wise philosopher") receives a response from Jesus, but the disciple Thomas's claim that he is incapable of comparing Jesus to anything results in further dialogue.

> Jesus said, "I am not your master. Because you have drunk, you have become intoxicated from the bubbling spring which I have measured out."
> And He took him and withdrew and told him three things. When Thomas returned to his companions, they asked him, "What did Jesus say to you?"
> Thomas said to them, "If I tell you one of the things which he told me, you will pick up stones and throw them at me; a fire will come out of the stones and burn you up."

After Peter identifies Jesus as the Christ in Mark 8:29, Jesus responds by charging the disciples "to tell no one about him" (v. 30)—a charge which the text itself apparently violates. In Mark 9:9, following the transfiguration, Jesus instructs Peter, James, and John to "tell no one what they had seen, except when (*ei mē hotan*) the son of man should rise up from the dead." Given Mark's treatment of the son of man and of the resurrection, this further "clarification" hardly addresses the difficulty presented at 8:30; indeed, the disciples question "what it might mean to rise from the dead" in the next verse (9:10). In Thomas 13, the purported author of the book, the one who "wrote down" the "secret sayings which the living Jesus spoke" (according to its introduction), refuses to tell others what Jesus said. The texts at these points announce their incompleteness, their own secrecy and the failure of that secrecy.

In Mark, Jesus proceeds to teach the disciples "frankly" (*parrēsiq9*) about the son of man's forthcoming passion, which makes paradoxical Peter's identification of Jesus as the messiah. The dialogue leads to Peter's rebuke of Jesus and then to Jesus's counter-rebuke: "Go behind me, Satan; because you do not think the thoughts of God, but of men" (8:33). Does Jesus not want the disciples to identify him as the Christ to others because they (especially Peter) are *wrong*? In contrast to the dialogue in Mark 3, Jesus and Satan are here clearly opposed, as are the sides of God (who is aligned with suffering and death and with the son of man) and of man (aligned with the messiah).

Given the later role of Peter as a traitor, can these harsh words of Jesus in Mark be unlike those words to which Thomas 13 refers—words which lead to stones and fire? Both accounts end in astonishment and uncertainty; in Thomas as in Mark, the disciples fail to understand. In the near lack of response in Mark and the unknown response to an inability to identify him in Thomas, the identity of Jesus remains indeterminate. Mark 8:31 tends in the direction of the marvelous: the resurrection of the son of man is foretold. However, in Mark, the relation between Jesus and the son of man is not one of simple identity.[10]

In Matthew's parallel (16:13–23) to Mark, Jesus responds much more positively to Peter, ascribing his confession to divine revelation and charging the disciples "to tell no one that he was the Christ." The change in the wording of Jesus's response results in a major clarification of who he is. Matthew's stress on Peter's role in the church (16:18–19) belongs to the larger Matthean agenda, but Jesus's rebuke that Peter is a hindrance to him would appear to contradict this. However, the problem of identity (both Jesus's and Peter's) has been resolved in this passage. Luke's version of the story (9:18–21) also confirms the identity of Jesus. Peter confesses that Jesus is "the Christ of God," to which Jesus replies by commanding the disciples "to tell this to no one." Following Jesus's passion prediction, there is no exchange of rebukes in Luke, which also removes the juxtaposition of identification and harsh words.

John's version of the dialogue (6:67–71) is characteristically unique. Peter says, "You have the words of everlasting life. . . . you are the holy one of God," to which Jesus replies that "one of you is an enemy."[11] John tells the reader that this refers to Judas; again the paradoxical conjunction (or non-disjunction) of identification and condemnation is resolved meta-textually, although the opposition of Jesus and Satan (as in Mark and Matthew) is retained. As in Mark and Thomas, however, the identity of Jesus remains undetermined.

In the synoptic gospels, when Pilate interrogates him regarding his identity as "King of the Jews," Jesus replies with the cryptic, "It is you who say it." Jesus makes no further reply to Pilate's questions. Although verbally identical in each of these gospels, the ambiguous reply acquires slightly different meanings in them, to the degree that Jesus's response to Peter's confession (among other textual clues) has already helped the reader to resolve the uncertainty of who Jesus really is. Hence this statement which in Mark's version is an enigmatic refusal to engage in further dialogue heaps irony upon Pilate's own irony in both Matthew's and Luke's stories.

In contrast, in John Jesus speaks at length with Pilate concerning the nature of his kingdom (18:29–38), establishing a theme which continues to operate through the first half of John 19. Jesus distinguishes sharply between his kingdom and "this world" in language not unlike Thomas (e.g., saying 80) but not identical to it, either. Jesus claims that he is to "testify" (*martureō*) to the truth. Thus in a sense the question is answered ("I am a king") but in a way that transforms the indeterminacy instead of eliminating it ("not of/from the world").

4. *The Synoptic Apocalypse.*

Three sayings in the Gospel of Thomas discuss the recognition of Jesus and the coming of the kingdom (37, 91, 113; cf. sayings 51 and 52). In each case the question about a future event is redirected by an answer focusing on present situations; Jesus is revealed "when you disrobe without being ashamed"; he is "this moment" which his interrogators "do not know how to read." In these sayings the kingdom

> will not come by waiting for it. It will not be a matter of saying "Here it is" or "There it is." Rather, the Kingdom of the Father is spread out upon the earth, and men do not see it. (see also Luke 17:20–21)

These themes also appear in the "synoptic apocalypse," Jesus's address to his disciples concerning the destruction of the temple and the end of the world (Mark 13:5–37 par.). In these texts, however, what is described is not "spread out upon the earth" at present, but something that is to come, and the signs are not about us now, waiting to be read by the wise, but strange events which have not yet occurred. The disciples are warned against "false Christs and false prophets" (Mark 13:22, Matt 7:15), and they are given various clues whereby the coming of the end can be forecast through both natural and historical phenomena.[12]

In each of the synoptic accounts appear the words, "this generation will not pass by before all these things are done" (Mark 13:30 par.), suggesting an expectation that the end will come while some of Jesus's auditors are still alive. These words are followed in each gospel by the statement, "The sky and the earth will pass away but my words will not pass away." In Matthew and Mark this statement is then followed by the claim that only "the father" knows when the end will come, and by warnings in all three gospels to remain alert and watchful, unless the end come upon one like an absent lord (Mark and Matthew), like a burglar (Matthew; see also Gos. Thom. 21, 103), or like a trap (Luke).

However, if Jesus's words "this generation" never pass away, then the end has been indefinitely deferred, for each generation which is addressed by them becomes "this generation." The immutable words disrupt the tension between the present and the eschaton. Any generation could be "this generation," and every generation must read "this moment" to see if it is *this* moment. The signs in the synoptic apocalypse point into the future, like the fig tree putting forth leaves, but the signs will be present signs or else they cannot be read. These sentences with their reinforcing texts, such as the parable of the doorkeeper (Mark 13:34–36), collapse the eschatological tension of the synoptic gospels into the present search in Thomas for "the interpretation of these sayings" (sayings 1 and 2; see also Mark 4:22, 13:37).

"My words will not pass away," not because they are the eternal, heavenly Logos, for that concept is foreign to the synoptic gospels, nor because they are the spoken words of the "living Jesus" (Thomas), for those words have passed away, but because they are the written, incarnate words of a text which although it has suffered much has not yet passed away. The independence of the written text from every generation allows "this generation" to be (perhaps) this generation, and this continually regenerates the need for interpretation.

The text requires a hermeneutical supplement; these signs which are about "reading the signs" must themselves be read. Unlike the book of Daniel, cited by Mark at 13:14, 19, 26, and elsewhere, Jesus refuses to announce the precise time of the end; that would be to presume to know what only God knows. Although the signs of the end seem quite specific, they must be read properly, or else one may be misled and destroyed. The synoptic apocalypse concludes in fantastic undecidability, a return from "that day" and "that hour" to "this moment" and this world, an escape from the apocalyptic escape, for "no one knows" (Mark 13:32).

It is the irony of apocalyptic, which so far as I know is an exclusively literary form,[13] that its announcement of the end occurs within the endlessness of the written text. As theorists from Aristotle to Kermode have stressed, there is a teleology in all narrative, a movement toward finality and closure which is built into the sequence of words itself, and of which the apocalypse is perhaps the most explicit form. Yet there is also in all literature a counter-current, a "spatial form"[14] which is linked to the physical medium itself: the spoken word is irreversible and irrevocable, but the reader can skip about in the written text and rearrange it, and this undermines and disrupts its teleology. The text is always fragmentary, incomplete.

In the aside of Mark 13:14, "let him who reads this take note of it," the text refers to itself as written.[15] However, unlike each spoken word which comes eventually to silence, every writing is the indefinite deferral of an end. In these passages, the spatiality of text, which is most explicit in the gospel of Thomas, does precisely that to the teleology of the synoptic apocalypse. For that teleology to be maintained, it must be "rescued" by a supplementary commentary, and Christian theology has been attempting to provide that for nearly two thousand years.

All of the synoptic accounts contain the paradox of "my words" (*hoi . . . logoi mou*) and "this generation" (*hē genea hautē*), and Matthew and Luke have not de-fantasized the Markan saying as they do so often elsewhere. Perhaps this is because these words are explicitly about the preservation of Jesus's words—that is, about the text itself. The words of Jesus are for these gospels written words, despite the narrative depiction of oral performance.

In Mark 8:38, in the midst of a paradoxical saying about discipleship which links Peter's confession and Jesus's rebuke to the transfiguration, the reader again finds the association of "my words" (*tous emous logous*) and "this . . . generation" (*tē geneą tautē*) again in a context of eschatological judgment: the next verse, Mark 9:1 (see also 13:30 par.), strongly suggests an immanent eschaton. These are conjoined in Mark 8:35 to "the gospel" (*tou euaggeliou*); Mark again refers to itself.[16] Here, however, the parallel accounts transform both the signifier and its context; Matthew 10:33 relocates the parallel and drops both sets of terms, and Luke 9:26 keeps "my words" but drops "this generation." These texts do not clearly refer to themselves—the reference to "the gospel" has disappeared—and the paradox has been eliminated from them.

5. Conclusion.

We cannot dispense with the metaphysical security of a mythic enclosure—a self-consistent, complete, and therefore "real" world—no matter how illusory or totalitarian it may be.[17] We require a hermeneutics to take otherwise meaningless objects or events and transform them into meaningful experience, a life, a story. That hermeneutics, whatever form it takes, is an incomplete and violent struggle for authority over a submissive yet resistant "text" (the as-yet uninterpreted object or event). The fantastic is the point at which that struggle is revealed for what it is.

The literary fantastic is prominent and significant at the levels of the Jesus traditions represented by Thomas and by Mark, and this fantastic element is gradually but decisively eliminated or neutralized by gospels such as Matthew and Luke, as the traditions are stabilized and an institutionalized orthodoxy begins to emerge in the Christian movement. This does not necessarily mean that the fantastic elements in the gospels originated with the actual man Jesus; fantastic narratives can readily be found in both Jewish and Gentile writings contemporary with or earlier than the gospels. Furthermore, another early stratum of the traditions, represented by the sayings source Q, consists largely of non-fantastic material.[18]

It is more likely that Matthew and Luke took fantastical narrative material from Mark or Thomas (or similar sources) and de-fantasized it, sometimes in different generic "directions," than it is that Mark or Thomas took relatively non-fantastical material and gave to it a fantastic twist. If either of them had done this, then a new subgenre would have emerged. According to Eric Rabkin, genres do undergo fantastic reversals of established ground-rules from time to time, and thus the fantastic plays an important role in both the formation and the evolution of genres. This role, however, is not a function of belief but of its opposite—the need for creativity and novelty.

By de-fantasizing the narrative, Matthew and Luke sought to make the Jesus story believable. This de-fantasizing tendency remains an important factor in Christian theology to the present, and it accounts in large part for the inability of many readers to recognize the fantastic in the gospels. The fantastic elements in Thomas and Mark have survived despite, not because of, the theological needs and influence of their readers. In fact, Thomas nearly did not survive, and Mark has always been the least popular of the canonical gospels. Mark's inclusion in the canon (and therefore its survival) probably had more to do with the high value that the church placed on Matthew and Luke than on any qualities of its own.

John presents a different case, for John apparently achieved that which Mark and Thomas could not. While John continued to draw upon the fantastic, it did so in a way that did not block faith but rather encouraged it. John re-fantasized that which had been de-fantasized by Matthew and Luke, and in this development the fantastic elements became more subtle but also less likely to interfere with the reader's search for reference to reality (= belief). The fantastic uncertainty which lies on the surface of Thomas's and Mark's discourse material, and which Matthew and Luke tend to dissolve in narrative followability and explicit christology, re-emerges in John as a "deep structure" of the fundamental conceptual framework which determines the narrative. "In the beginning was the Word" became a creed, not a paradox. John neutralized the fantastic, not by eliminating it but by giving it a mythic context which made it safe for orthodox Christian belief.

NOTES

1. "Poverty and the Hermeneutics of Repentance," *Cross Currents* (Winter, 1988–89), "Literary Fantasy and the Composition of the Gospels," *Forum* (September, 1989), "The Fantastic in the Parabolic Language of Jesus," *Neotestamentica* (Spring, 1990), and "Biblical Miracle Narratives as Fantasy," in *Anglican Theological Review* (Winter, 1991).

2. The connection with almsgiving is not clear. The first half of Thomas 14 appears to be a reply to a question asked by the disciples in Thomas 6; compare Matthew 6:2–18. See also Thomas 22: "when you make the inside like the outside and the outside like the inside . . . then you will enter" the kingdom, and Thomas 89.

3. In the version of the citation of Isaiah in Matthew 13:10–17, parables are used "because" (*hoti*) the crowds do not believe, rather than "so that" (*hina*) they may not believe, as in Mark 4:10–13 (also vv. 33–34) (Kermode:29–33). Jesus again cites Isaiah just prior to the discourse on the mouth, at Mark 7:6b–7 par.

4. I discuss the fantastic elements in Thomas 22 and 98 in "The Fantastic in the Parabolic Language of Jesus."

5. Lattimore translates *hoi par' autou* in 3:21 with these words; NRSV translates them as "his family." Later, Jesus speaks privately to *hoi peri auton sun tois dodeka* (Mark 4:10). Lattimore translates this as "his followers along with the twelve"; NRSV translates "those who were around him along with the twelve."

6. Compare also Matt. 12:32 and Luke 12:10. Note that the "sons of men" who are forgiven in Mark apparently become the "son of man" who is blasphemed in Matthew and Luke.

7. Likewise, in the parable collection of Matthew 13, only the parables of the treasure and of the pearl remain free of explicit or implicit allegorization, as comparison with the parallels in Mark or Thomas makes clear.

8. See the insightful comments of Temma Berg (197–98).

9. This is the only time that *parrēsia* appears in Mark. The word suggests the bold frankness of a Cynic teacher, in sharp contrast to the otherwise enigmatic, parabolic Jesus of Mark. *Parrēsia* is not used at all in Matthew or Luke, but appears nine times in John.

10. Contrast Matthew 16:13 and 15, where Jesus's parallel questions to the disciples make the equation Jesus = son of man quite explicit. The nearest Mark comes to anything like this is in 14:41–42.

11. According to Lattimore's translation. The NRSV translates the Greek *diabolos* with the more evident (but theologically more "loaded") "devil." Might *diabolos* have something in common with *skandalon* (RSV: "hindrance") in Matthew 16:23, as Lattimore's translation suggests?

12. Compare Thomas 79 to Mark 13:17 par.

13. An oral apocalypse is not inconceivable, but as a narrative form, the apocalypse occurs in literate cultures. Apocalyptic emerges in post-exilic Judaism at the very time that the acceptance of the written Torah and the written collections of sayings of the prophets and the wise become increasingly important. The post-exilic prophets and apocalypses refer frequently to writings, scrolls, etc. This is not a coincidence.

14. The best statement on spatial form remains Joseph Frank's essay, "Spatial Form in Modern Literature" (1963).

15. Sandmel notes that Mark 7:1–8 (see above) is a rejection of the oral Torah in favor of the written Torah (32). The gospel of Thomas also explicitly refers to itself as written.

16. Whether or not Mark uses the term "gospel" as a designation for itself, "gospel" appears to be associated with Mark's text—more explicitly at 1:1 and perhaps 14:9. The opposition in these verses between losing one's life "for the sake of me and the gospel" and being ashamed "of me and my words" (and thereby earning the shame of the son of man) is quite provocative.

17. Perhaps no one has described the nature or the mechanisms of this desire for the readable better than Roland Barthes did, throughout the entirety of his writings but especially in *S/Z*.

18. See "The Fantastic in the Parabolic Language of Jesus." Q and the gospel of Thomas resemble one another as sayings collections (*logoi sophon*) and contain many sayings in common, but there are important theological differences between them. The fantastic plays a significant role in these differences. Likewise, Mark's "son of man" sayings are more indeterminate generically than are Q's. See also Tina Pippin's study of the fantastic in the Apocalypse of John in this volume. Crossan's recent analyses of the gospel of Peter indicate that the early, pre-synoptic stratum of Peter identified by Crossan contains a great deal of fantastic material. The Pauline writings appear to be largely non-fantastic, but this needs further examination.

WORKS CONSULTED

Berg, Temma F.
    1989   "Reading In/To Mark." *Semeia* 48:187–206.

Cameron, Ron, ed.
    1982   *The Other Gospels*. Philadelphia: Westminster.

Crossan, John Dominic
    1988   *The Cross That Spoke*. San Francisco: Harper and Row.

Frank, Joseph
    1963   *The Widening Gyre*. New Brunswick: Rutgers University Press.

Jeremias, Joachim
    1963   *The Parables of Jesus*. Trans. S. H. Hooke. London: SCM.

Kermode, Frank
    1979   *The Genesis of Secrecy*. Cambridge: Harvard University Press.

Lattimore, Richmond, trans.
    1979   *The Four Gospels and the Revelation*. New York: Dorset.

Rabkin, Eric S.
    1976   *The Fantastic in Literature*. Princeton: Princeton University Press.

Sandmel, Samuel
    1978   *Anti-Semitism in the New Testament?* Philadelphia: Fortress.

Todorov, Tzvetan
    1973   *The Fantastic: A Structural Approach to a Literary Genre*. Trans. Richard Howard. Cleveland: Case Western Reserve University Press.

THE HEROINE AND THE WHORE: FANTASY AND THE FEMALE IN THE APOCALYPSE OF JOHN[1]

Tina Pippin
Agnes Scott College

ABSTRACT

The female figures of the Heroine and the Whore are the basic archetypes for women in the Apocalypse of John. Using fantasy and science fiction theory, the literary function of the female in the text is explored. The fantastic representation of the female in the Apocalypse has hermeneutical implications for women readers past and present. Fantasy studies show the text as subversive and political and also as a dangerous, unliberating text for women.

---

1. Introduction.

In responding to science fiction writer Joanna Russ, Robert Scholes states, "Maybe an all-female world is the only hope for the future of the human race. It's worth considering." (Scholes:87). Women readers of the Apocalypse of John may entertain a similar idea. In the Apocalypse the earth-bound females (Jezebel and the Whore of Babylon) are immoral and seductive and help the evil men in the destruction of earth. Only the Woman Clothed with the Sun is able to function positively in bringing about the utopia, but even she is left out of the utopian city (represented by the Bride). The role of the female is subordinate in the text; once women are used or abused there is no further need for them in the future world or their future function is left undefined.

Reading the text as a woman demands reading for the gender codes in the narrative where women appear or are noticeably absent. If Joanna Russ is correct in her analysis of science fiction, there are no women, only "images of women." The female in fantasy literature is also an image; in the Apocalypse this image is blurred or stereotyped when present or absent altogether. Women are either on "the edge of time" (to borrow from Marge Piercy) or completely displaced from time.

In the enchanting and disenchanting world of the Apocalypse of John the role of the female is overlooked. This displacement occurs in the political and religious sphere. But women are displaced twice—they are "double-bound" to subordinate roles in both worlds. The apocalyptic text reveals and displaces two main female archetypes: the Heroine (queen-mother of heaven) figure and the Whore (Babylon-queen-mother of hell). Studies in fantasy literature and folk and fairy tales provide interesting parallels to the apocalyptic imagination. The subversive text of the Apocalypse subverts the status quo without changing the gender relations and empowering the "collective female."

2. *The Function of the Female in the Apocalypse.*

Women are most noticeably absent in the Apocalypse in 14:4: "It is these who have not defiled themselves with women, for they are virgins." The 144,000 represent the whole number of the faithful, and they are men. Adela Yarbro Collins (1987:84-90) notices that this passage employs sacrificial language and reflects purity laws. Women's bodies are seen as negative and capable of defiling the men. Yarbro Collins hints that this passage "assumes that the model Christian is male" (1987:90), but she fails to make full use of the logical inference—that the New Jerusalem, God's future world, will exclude females! For the candidates for heaven to remain "spotless"—indeed for heaven itself to remain spotless—women are displaced. "And in their mouth no lie was found; they are blameless" in 14:5 removes the power of discourse from women. Male is the subject; female is the object—the object of desire that must be displaced.

Thus, the subject-object split is in place—that same split that is the dialectic of body/mind, nature/culture, and male/female. Gayatri Spivak says of this split that in order to make the female subject, "The collective project of our feminist critique must always be to rewrite the *social* text so that the historical and sexual differentials are operated together" (1983:185). In the Apocalypse the narrative as "socially symbolic act" (Jameson) retains the sexual oppression and stereotypes of woman as object of violence and desire. A feminist hermeneutic rereads the narrative for its gender codes. A key question is who is the female and what are her powers and plays in the Apocalypse?

A tension exists in the narrative between the archetypes of the female. This dialectic of archetypal material can be explained by the subject-object split or in terms of binary oppositions or by the concept of displacement. Spivak's concern is with the concept of difference and in particular, sexual difference, which is of course out of her reading of Derridean deconstruction. The female that is displaced as subject in this political fantasy is the female that reflects (mirrors or mimics) aspects of the prevailing social order (both good and evil) and ideology.

Lance Olsen's definition of postmodern fantasy clarifies the deconstructive mode of fantasy literature:

> Often fantasy begins in the realm of the mimetic, then disrupts it introducing an element of the marvelous, the effect being to jam marvelous and mimetic assumptions. In other words, fantasy is that stutter between two modes of discourse which generates textual instability, an ellipse of uncertainty . . . its result is the banging together of the *here* and *there* so that neither the reader nor the protagonist knows quite where he is. That is, fantasy is a deconstructive mode of narrative. (19)
> Hence, the fantastic is a mode designed to surprise, to question, to put into doubt, to create anxiety, to make active, to make uncomfortable, to disgust, to repel, to rebel, to subvert, to pervert, to make ambiguous, to make discontinuous, to deform. It is a mode whose premise is a will to deconstruct. (22)

The Apocalypse has elements of both the supernatural (Todorov's "marvelous") and the mimetic. And the narrative certainly subverts the "reality" of political domination. But the images of the female remain the same as in the dominant society—only in the reverse; the images are turned inside-out. If Rosemary Jackson is correct in saying, "The fantastic traces the unsaid and the unseen of culture: that which has been silenced, made invisible, covered over and made 'absent'" (4), then the Apocalypse falls short of complete subversion of the social order. The female is still absent, even though she is represented in both powerful and powerless modes of being and acting. The female is still other, still marginalized, still banished to the edges of the text.

Females in the Apocalypse are few but noticeable, and their future is prophesied. The prophetess Jezebel and her unrepentant followers will be thrown upon a bed and will die (2:22-23). The Whore of Babylon is dethroned and made desolate and totally destroyed, as the ceremonial lines proclaim: "Fallen, fallen is Babylon the great!" (18:2). Even the Woman Clothed with the Sun is "banished" for protection and safekeeping to the wilderness "to her place where she is nourished for a time, and times, and half a time" (12:14). The female becomes the absent cause—the cause of both evil and good—but nonetheless is erased from the text. The bride image (the New Jerusalem) alone is left standing, but only briefly; she is replaced by the imagery of the city. The final female image is connected with a male, the Lamb, and described as "prepared as a bride adorned for her husband" (21:2). The Bride is woman as object, adorned and passive; the New Jerusalem is the image of the seductive, the object of erotic desire. I want to show that all the females in the Apocalypse are victims; they are objects of desire and violence because they are all stereotyped, archetypal images of the female and not the embodiment of power and control over their own lives or the real or fantastic worlds.

The language of female subjection and displacement in the Apocalypse comes out of the unconscious. And the unconscious is part of the imaginary order. Imagination is not fixed but fluid. The unconscious desire for the new social and political order does nothing to improve the status of women. The imaginary is ideological (Althusser), and the ideology of gender types in the text are controlled by the sexual imagination of the male. The imagination operating in the text involves the image of the virginal male controlling the female images because of the hierarchal order of God and the Lamb, the 144,000, the good female images, and the evil female images and those males who are seduced by them. The desire of the true believer is to enter the heavenly city (the Bride). But there is erotic tension at this point; there is distancing from the female; entrance into the female is future and is possible only if the group of men desiring her remain sexually pure and undefiled by women. The vision is real; the world of the unreal becomes real in fantasy literature.

Studies on women in traditional science fiction have revealed the powerlessness of women in the future world. The male remains the paradigm and subject of the future. One such study relates that women function as sexual beings and "as appropriate rewards for the male protagonists who solve the problem. When a woman acts independently, she is evil; when she has power, it is intuitive or magical; when she has extrahuman abilities, they are the problem" (Allen and Paul:171). The granting of magical abilities in the Apocalypse must come from God or the Lamb; women who act on their own are defying the male defined sex roles for women. Thus, the Jezebel and the Whore are destroyed, but the real point is that these autonomous females are used as "scapegoats" for the evil in society. Evil is again associated with the female and with her body.

The female with power is both desired and feared. The threat of a female with power over men—power identified in the form of seduction—is so feared that the reaction is violence against the female. Unconscious (or conscious) desire for the powerful, autonomous female remains even after she is destroyed. The image is still implanted on men's minds; in the Apocalypse the desire is transferred to the Bride. Coming out of the Whore and entering the Bride is set up as a rite of undefiled men, but the sexual fantasy is strong and luring. The Bride lures the 144,000; the adorned Bride is an enchanting and erotic image. All the apocalyptic females are erotic images with erotic power over men.

The erotic, enchanting female brings either death or birth. The either-or nature of the political stance in the Apocalypse is clear, but here I want to further this claim to the sexual images. The distinct female archetypes represents either the way to God (rebirth in the New Jerusalem) or the way to Satan (death in the abyss). Donald Palumbo makes an interesting point about the "connection between eroticism and death." Our subconscious fears of the unknown (especially death) are made available to us in fantasy literature; fantasy overcomes death (4). Palumbo believes that the concern of the fantastic with sexuality gives it "psychological appeal." He summarizes his findings: "And sexuality almost always appears as the symbolic vehicle of rebirth in the nearly ubiquitous death and resurrection motifs that suffuse great fantasy literature" (23). Fear of imperialism, fear of famine, fear of disease, fear of death itself are infused into the archetype of the seductive Whore whose erotic power over men is the most terrifying in a society that marginalizes and depowers females. Females with autonomous power bring death. Only those females who are connected with God—adorned for the honeymoon or with wombs for use by God—that is, brides and mothers (men-identified women) are safe. These are women who are controlled by men and who do not exercise their powers on their own. Still, they, too, lure men; they are also highly erotic images of desire. And the archetypes of bride and queen-mother are intended to be more erotic, more desirable and enchanting than the archetypes of prophetess and whore.

3. *The Heroine.*

The Woman Clothed with the Sun in Apocalypse 12 is so historicized that she has almost lost her place as a character in her own right in the story. Like the Bride and the Whore who represent cities, she is seen as representing institutions; i.e., Israel and the Church. But unlike the other female figures in the text, the Woman Clothed with the Sun has no name. Her fate is undetermined (although we assume she is safe), whereas the fate of the others is explicitly stated. She is set against a formidable foe, the great red dragon, but with help (from God) she is able to escape. She is speechless except for her cries of pain in childbirth. And she is overlooked—barely visible—since traditionally the battle between God and Satan has overshadowed her importance in the text.

If readings of the Grimms' *Kinder-und Haus Märchen* and other folk and fairy tales are any indication, then the reader's identification (especially if the reader is a woman) is with the heroine in a story. Karen Rowe offers an explanation for this heroine identification:

> Thus, subconsciously women may transfer from fairy tales into real life cultural norms which exalt passivity, dependency, and self-sacrifice as a female's cardinal virtues. In short, fairy tales perpetuate the patriarchal *status quo* by making female subordination seem a romantically desirable, indeed an inescapable fate. (1979:237)

The implication of this mother archetype is that the female as a sexual being is affirmed only in the act of giving birth (to the messiah, no less!). In other words, the message is that females are productive when they are reproductive. The woman in Apocalypse 12 is identified twice by her reproductive event (12:5 and 13). The sexual affirmation of the Heroine in the birth process is in direct opposition to the orgy of the Whore and her followers.² Pain in childbirth is set against the pleasure of orgasm (see Spivak on Derrida on orgasm as crime, 175). Sexual difference in the text points out the dialectic of desire; the text plays with the erotic on both sides (good and evil females) while reaffirming traditional stereotypes of the good woman who is obedient and long-(emphasis on long) suffering.

In Apocalypse 12 the woman is connected with nature. Sun and moon and stars and wilderness evoke the natural order but also open the way to God. Adela Yarbro Collins finds parallels between the Queen of Heaven in Apocalypse 12 and the goddesses Artemis (Ephesus), Atargatis (Syria), and especially Isis (Egypt and Asia Minor). Sun, moon, and stars (zodiac) are used in depictions of these goddesses. Yarbro Collins states, "The astral attributes with which she is endowed seem to belong to the typical depiction of a high goddess" (1976:75). Another detail of the goddess Isis that is shared by the woman in 12:14 is the giving of the wings. Isis is represented in the form of a swallow who has power in flight. A typical image of the goddess is this bird motif. The magical wings enable the woman to escape danger and fly to the wilderness. The bird motif is a very powerful symbol of the high goddess, but the woman is not allowed to be a powerful high goddess. The Whore is high goddess for a while, but she is brought down by the male god. Here is another example, like the grotesque destruction of Tiamat in the Enuma Elish, of the death of the goddess and the replacement of the male god as head.

The Heroine in this story does not get enough credit. She gives birth on her own to the messiah child, who is immediately snatched from her by God and taken up to heaven. Meanwhile, the woman flees to the wilderness two times (12:6 and 14), and she is left in the wilderness. She enacts a kind of "travelling heroism" that is evident in women characters of fantasy literature (Lefanu:ch. 3) and is an active heroine, except that she does not enact her own equality (Maclean:45). She takes the initiative in fleeing to the wilderness and is taken care of by God. The Woman Clothed with the Sun is a goddess subdued, tamed, and under control. After her reproductive activity she is no longer useful. The traditional female values that accompany the act of mothering (nurture and caretaking) are suppressed; the child is taken to live in heaven, and traditional male values of competition and separation come to the foreground. The Heroine, Jezebel, and the Whore are all three hunted; only the Heroine escapes, but her escape is banishment from the center of power. The female is decentered even when it is held as an ideal woman.

Why the residue of the goddess—Queen of Heaven cults? If the woman in Apocalypse 12 is the producer of the one who will liberate the oppressed, then why is she not herself liberated? The irony of the function of women in the Apocalypse is incredible. The Queen of Heaven is condemned to silence.

Silence has an interesting function for the females of the Apocalypse. The model of the silent woman is a model for many heroines in fantasy and folktale. According to Eugene Weber, "... it is not surprising that in a lot of folktales enduring in silence is one of the most common tests a heroine (or even a hero) has to pass, often connected with torment by witches or by devils" (110). Ruth Bottigheimer finds that the majority of folktales in *Grimms' Tales* condemn "women to silence during which they are often exposed to mortal danger" (1987:71), which is part of what Bottigheimer refers to as "textual silence and powerlessness" (1987:53).[3] The Heroine of Apocalypse 12 "cried out in her pangs of birth"; we hear her anguish but not her words. Instead of words, she is given wings, "the two wings of the great eagle" (12:13). Still, she does not speak; she endures in silence in the wilderness. The two brief scenes of power where she flees and flies into the wilderness are quickly joined with scenes of dependency on the power of God as the ultimate protection. She is a goddess who has some power but needs to be saved by the male God to keep that power in control.

The textual/sexual strategies at work in the motif of the silent female are dangerous to women's consciousness. Female voice and values are suppressed. Marcia Landy (27) summarizes the problem:

> ... for the most part women have concurred, have accepted the male images as their own or have created accommodations satisfactory to them within the given power structure—a Virgin Queen, an Amazon, a Wielder of Power over Children and Lovesick Men—or women have agreed to see themselves as witches, demons, and deceivers. The consequences of straying from legitimized social norms were obviously too costly to entertain—deprivation of God, of man, of sociability, of economic sustenance, of biological needs.

Political and economic structures are subverted in the Apocalypse, but women's roles and functions remain the same. The woman who "speaks," Jezebel, is vicious not virtuous. The archetyping of the female and her narrative silence relay a powerful message to the reader/hearer of the text: all women are to remain silent, but not all silent women are "good."

4. *The Whore.*

In the Hebrew Bible the harlot is sometimes characterized as a heroine (Tamar in Gen 38; Rahab in Josh 2 & 6). But the loose woman of the Proverbs is depicted as a deceiver and a foreigner. In the Apocalypse the Whore, whose name on her forehead (a sign of slavery) is Babylon, is the "mother of harlots and of earth's abominations" (17:5). She is the ultimate deceiver and "loose woman." The Whore is seductive; she is adorned in fine clothes and jewels and sits upon a scarlet beast. But when one looks closer, the golden cup is full of the evil of her sexual acts with the kings of the earth. And she is "drunk with the blood of the saints and the blood of the witnesses of Jesus" (18:6). The scene of the Whore is extremely grotesque; she is a huge, exaggerated presence who is "seated on many waters" (17:1). As in chapter 12 the setting for this vision is the wilderness, but in this scene the female is brutally murdered.

The thoughts of the Whore are revealed in 18:7: "Since in her heart she says, 'I rule as a queen; I am no widow, and I will never see grief.'" The belief in and expression of the powers of women are remnants of ancient belief in the Mother Goddess. Bottigheimer comments, "the female's original access to power through her association with nature became perverted and denied, so that more recent versions of fairy tales [e.g., the Grimms'] relegate power held by females to the old, the ugly, and/or the wicked" (1980:12). The Whore declares herself (to herself) a queen, and because of her egoism she is judged and destroyed.

The destruction of the Whore is violent and total destruction. This fantastic scene is played on a grand scale; this scene is a "parody" of the social, political, economic, and religious system. The dialogical model of Mikhail Bakhtin is useful in reading this fantastic "parody". As Rosemary Jackson summarizes:

> Unlike the marvelous or the mimetic, the fantastic is a mode of writing which *enters a dialogue with the 'real' and incorporates that dialogue as part of its essential structure.* To return to Bakhtin's phrase, fantasy is 'dialogical', interrogating single or unitary ways of seeing. (36)

Bakhtin's formalist ties show that language is subversive; the dominant ideology is "interrogated" in fantasy. The form (genre) of this use of language is the Menippean satire, which Bakhtin finds as an example of parody. By parody Bakhtin means, "the creation of a *decrowning double*; it is that same 'world turned inside out' . . . it was like an entire system of crooked mirrors, elongating, diminishing, distorting in various directions and to various degrees" (127). Bakhtin finds menippea in the New Testament (gospels, Acts, and Apocalypse) but notes that the "dialogic element of the menippea" is expressed in the relations of opposites (good and evil) and thereby managed (135). Parody is located in the genre of the carnivalesque. The carnival is used in folklore to express a "serio-comical" approach to the world (108). Bakhtin reveals three main characteristics of the genre of the serio-comical: (1) the time of the narrative is the present reality; (2) the narrative is based on history and not legend, relying on "experience . . . and on free invention"; (3) the narrative has multiple levels, or in Bakhtin's words:

> Characteristic of these genres are a multi-tone narration, the mixing of high and low, serious and comic; they make wide use of inserted genres—letters, found manuscripts, retold dialogues, parodies on the high genres, parodically reinterpreted citations; in some of them we observe a mixing of prosaic and poetic speech, living dialects and jargons . . . are introduced, and various authorial masks make their appearance. . . . And what happens here, as a result, is a radically new relationship to the word as the material of literature. (108)

This "carnival sense of the world" as both comic and serious is found in Christian narrative. Bakhtin gives the example of "the scene of crowning and decrowning" Jesus as King of the Jews in the Gospel narratives (135). The scene of the fall of Babylon is also directly carnivalesque. The Whore all adorned on the scarlet beast and who considers herself a queen is dethroned. The narrator tells us of the erotic image of the Whore as queen: "When I saw her, I was greatly amazed" (17:6). This mock coronation/decoronation scene is a ritual event which is performed in the public square and streets and was a communal ritual (128). Bakhtin describes the significance of this ritual:

> Carnival is the festival of all-annihilating and all-renewing time . . . this is not an abstract thought but a living sense of the world, expressed in concretely sensuous forms (either expressed or play-acted) of the ritual act. Crowning/decrowning is a dualistic ambivalent ritual, expressing the inevitability and at the same time the creative power of the shift-and-renewal, the *joyful relativity* of all structure and order, of all authority and all (hierarchial) position. . . . Birth is fraught with death, and death with new birth. (124-125)

Through the carnival the masquerading queen is stripped of her power. The dominant ideology of power and oppression is overthrown in the carnival ritual. The mixture of poetry and prose provides a powerful sense of the eccentricity of the Whore and the shift of the structures of authority.

The horror the carnival death of the Whore is expressed in vivid terms: "And the ten horns that you saw, they and the beast will hate the whore; they will make her desolate and naked; they will devour her flesh and burn her up with fire" (17:16). Bakhtin finds the image of fire ambivalent in carnival: "It is a fire that simultaneously destroys and renews the world" (126). Three times (17:16; 18:8, 9) is her burning mentioned and once that she will burn forever (19:3); three times it is mentioned that the destruction occurs in one hour (18:10, 17, 19). In this scene the erotic tension is heightened; the Whore is literally stripped naked of her fine garments and jewels. Nakedness equals helplessness. Like the dragon goddess Tiamat in the Enuma Elish, the Whore is disembodied. The erotic tension here points to the ultimate misogynist fantasy! All the world's hatred of oppression is heaped on the Whore: "With such violence

Babylon the great city will be thrown down, and will be found no more" (18:21). The people at the carnival "devour her flesh" (17:16), and the violent feast image is repeated in chapter 19 when the birds of midheaven are called to "Come, gather for the great supper of God, to eat the flesh of kings, the flesh of captains, the flesh of the mighty, the flesh of horses and their riders, and the flesh of all, both free and slave, both small and great (vv. 17-18) . . . and all the birds were gorged with their flesh" (v. 21). These two grotesque feasts frame the marriage supper of the Lamb in 19:9. The menu of the marriage supper is not given.

Everything is turned inside out in this carnival: the Whore is "drunk with the blood of the saints and the blood of the witnesses of Jesus" (17:6 and 18:24), the nations are drunk from fornicating with the Whore, the nations in turn feast on the Whore's desolate body (and in the process lose all their delicacies [18:11-17], and finally, the birds of heaven feast on the nations.[4] With the death of the Whore the Bride "has made herself ready" (19:7) and "'to her it has been granted to be clothed with fine linen, bright and pure'—for the fine linen is the righteous deeds of the saints" (19:8). This rebirth after the death of the Whore is a sexual rebirth, or at least a rebirth in sexual imagery (the marriage feast). The witch is burned (the hunting of the Whore is a form of witch hunt), and the heroine image is finally free.

The Whore is totally seductive. The Whore totally dominates. In Apocalypse 18:4 a voice from heaven says, "Come out of her, my people, so that you do not take part in her sins, and so that you do not share in her plagues." The erotic power of the Whore is all-encompassing, for the people are asked to "come out of her." Then in 22:17 the word "come" is repeated to the believers: "The Spirit and the bride say, 'Come.' And let everyone who hears say, 'Come.' And let anyone who is thirsty come, let anyone who desires take the water of life as a gift." The believers who come out of the Whore are able in the end to enter the New Jerusalem, to "come" into the Bride. Richard Kearney explains Derrida's comment on the significance of the word, "come":

> 'Come' is a paradigmatic figure of postmodern apocalypse because it deconstructs every conceptual or linguistic attempt to *decide* what it means. It hails from an altogether *other* world. And what it puts into play is an apocalypse *without* apocalypse—since we cannot say or know or imagine what the 'truth' of apocalypse means. Derrida thus confronts us with the word of an apocalyptic writing which can only be grasped, if at all, as an *ending without end* . . . What is to come is, apparently, beyond the powers of imagination to imagine. (294-295)

The deconstructive play of apocalypse leaves the text open-ended and (temporally) shifts the object of desire (from the Whore to the Bride). The narrative itself is seductive, drawing the reader to the "ending without end"—the open spaces of the fantastic vision.

5. Conclusion.

The utopian political fantasy as a liberating, cathartic, revolutionary, symbolic experience is directly related to communal human experience. Liberation (materialist) readings of texts have always warned against such emphasis on the general (here, the cosmic), because oppression and marginalization are always specific, always personal. The female figures in the Apocalypse are given symbolic names and symbolic tasks; they are not allowed to speak their own identity. This technique distances the reader from the female images, leaving the women stereotypes of good and evil and not real flesh and blood women. But then the Apocalypse is about a symbolic universe and is a parody of flesh and blood reality. The female images are part of the larger paradigm of the final scenes in the liberation of the oppressed.

Yet this explanation is distorted, just as the image of the world of the dominant power is distorted (and thereby revealed) in the narrative. In the Christian utopia the expectations of power and authority are reversed—the beasts are defeated and the Lamb rules. At least the expectations for men are reversed; women are left exactly where they are in Mediterranean society—excluded from the realm of power. The utopia (no place) for men is an atopia (not a place) for women. The marriage of the Bride and the Lamb brings hope (brings utopia) but is not an inclusive model for women. Women have historically been excluded from many areas of culture, but are they also excluded in this text from the New Jerusalem? What happens to the female believers other than being subsumed under this image of the Bride? Here the text is silent.

In their anthropological study of female roles in culture, Judith Hoch-Smith and Anita Spring summarize the mythical representation of the female images: "The idea of female evil is transformed into specific cultural expression through *the manifestation of that culture's ideological content in art* . . . Female sexuality is seen as a disruptive, chaotic force that must be controlled or coopted by men, periodically purified, and at times destroyed" (3; emphasis mine). The ideology of the female in the Apocalypse remains true to the dominant ideology of its culture. But when women read the narrative (especially contemporary women readers), the experience is like the one delineated by Jonathan Culler: "When we posit a woman reader, the result is an analogous appeal to experience: not to the experience of girl-watching but to the experience of being watched, seen as a 'girl,' restricted, marginalized" (1982:44).

Women readers of the Apocalypse are typed, hunted, adorned, and rejected. The domination of male over female remains intact.

Fredric Jameson is correct on one level (that of the class struggle in history) when he points to the relationship of utopia and ideology: "ideological commitment is not first and foremost a matter of moral choice but of the taking of sides in a struggle between embattled groups . . . [and] must always necessarily be focused on the class enemy" (1981.290).5 But on the level of gender differences and conflict Jameson's analysis falls short. Ideology is also gender based and biased. The Apocalypse focuses on the class enemy (Rome) but neglects the oppressed/oppressor categories of gender relations. In the political realm women are defeated or banished to the wilderness; only the submissive, sexual Bride is allowed at the utopian feast of the Lamb. The image and the function of the female remains ambiguous: the erotic desire of the narrative is intact with the symbol of the Bride, but the men who enter her must be ritually pure, and the female figures with any sexual autonomy (the Jezebel, the Whore, and the Heroine share this feature) are pushed out or to the edge of the narrative.

If the writer of the Apocalypse is treated to the same gender critique as writers like Paul, Chaucer, and Rabelais, there will probably emerge defenders on both sides: those who defend the writer, "John," as "a man of his era" in which women were debased and powerless, and those who accuse and dismiss the writer as continuing sexist ideology which is of no use to women. A feminist reading can focus on the remnants of the goddess reflected in the winged flight of the Heroine and the murder of the Whore. Or a feminist reading can hope with Roland Barthes that the future will involve a destruction of the past "in which the potent seed of the future *is nothing but* the most profound apocalypse of the present" (157). The destruction of the past means the destruction of *all* the forces of oppression.

The Christian Apocalypse of John is limited in its destruction. The irony of the grotesque burning of the Whore is that the Christian utopia is itself an oppressive world (for women). In other words, for women there is no escaping oppression (except to flee to the wilderness?). Historically, the church eventually merges with the Roman state. And Christian women seek autonomy in the monastery (in the wilderness) in a sexually exclusive environment. But in the Apocalypse narrative gender oppression is left untouched by the sword of God.

The tale of the Heroine and the Whore is not a tale of the liberation of female consciousness. The Apocalypse is not a tale for women. The misogyny which underlies this narrative is extreme. Women of the past as well as the present are going to have to be about the business of creating their own apocalyptic tales, their own utopian narratives.

NOTES

1. This article is adapted from Tina Pippin, *Death and Desire: The Rhetoric of Gender in the Apocalypse of John* (Louisville: Westminster/John Knox, 1992).
2. Judith Hoch-Smith and Anita Spring provide a brief summary of "chaotic female sexuality." They state emphatically: "In no religious system do women's dominant metaphors derive from characteristics other than their sexual and reproductive status. . . . Women are strikingly one-dimensional characters in mythology and ritual action. Images of women are reduced to their sexual function, women are excluded from leadership roles in most public rituals, and images of the divine are usually male" (2).
3. Ruth Bottigheimer adds, "In *Grimms' Tales*, however, silence is almost exclusively female; enforced silence exists for both heroines and heroes as a precondition for redeeming oneself or others; and it also exists as a punishment for heroines (but not heroes) and as a narrative necessity for heroines (but not heroes), as in 'The Robber-Bridegroom' (1987:74-75). She also points to the Christian prohibition against female speech in 1 Cor 14:34-35 (1987:78). In another article Bottigheimer states that "one must conclude that fairy tales offered an apparently innocent and peculiarly suitable medium for both transmitting and enforcing the norm of the silent woman . . . serving as paradigms for powerlessness" (1986:130).
4. The juxtaposition of the feast on the Whore and the marriage feast of the lamb is described by Michael Harris (1988).
5. Jameson makes an interesting point about the semiological arrangement of the folktale: "the crucial moment for the folk tale is not that of the *parole*, . . . but that of the *langue* . . . it is always anonymous or collective in essence" (1972:29).

WORKS CONSULTED

Allen, V. and T. Paul
    1986   "Science and Fiction: Ways of Theorizing about Women." Pp. 165-183 in *Erotic Universe: Sexuality and Fantastic Literature*. Ed. Donald Palumbo. New York: Greenwood.

Althusser, Louis
    1969   *For Marx*. Trans. Ben Brewster. Harmondsworth: Penguin.

Bakhtin, Mikhail
    1984   *Problems of Dostoevsky's Poetics*. Ed. and trans. Caryl Emerson. Minneapolis: University of Minnesota Press.

Barthes, Roland
    1972   *Mythologies*. Trans. Annette Lavers. New York: Hill and Wang.

Bartkowski, Frances
    1987–88   "A Fearful Fancy: Some Reconsiderations of the Sublime." *Boundary 2* 15:23-32.

Bottigheimer, Ruth
    1987   *Grimms' Bad Girls & Bold Boys: The Moral & Social Vision of the Tales.* New Haven: Yale University Press.
    1986   "Silenced Women in the Grimms' Tales: The 'Fit' Between Fairy Tales and Society in Their Historical Context." Pp. 115-131 in *Fairy Tales and Society: Illusion, Allusion, and Paradigm.* Ed. Ruth Bottigheimer. Philadelphia: University of Pennsylvania Press.
    1980   "The Transformed Queen: A Search for the Origins of Negative Female Archetypes in Grimms' Fairy Tales." Pp. 1-12 in *Gestaltet und Gestaltend: Frauen in der Deutschen Literatur.* Ed. Marianne Burkhard. Amsterdam: Rodopi, N.V.

Brooke-Rose, Christine
    1981   *A Rhetoric of the Unreal: Studies in Narrative & Structure, Especially of the Fantastic.* Cambridge: Cambridge University Press.

Culler, Jonathan
    1973   "Literary Fantasy." *Cambridge Review* 95:30-33.
    1982   *On Deconstruction: Theory and Criticism after Structuralism.* Ithaca: Cornell University Press.

Darton, Robert
    1984   *The Great Cat Massacre and Other Episodes in French Cultural History.* New York: Basic Books.

Frappier-Mazur, Lucienne
    1988   "Marginal Canons: Rewriting the Erotic." *Yale French Studies* 75:112-128.

Galbreath, Robert
    1988   "Fantastic Literature as Gnosis." *Extrapolation* 29:330-337.

Harris, Michael A.
    1988   "Singing a New Song: The Literary Function of the Hymns in the Apocalypse of John." Ph.D. dissertation, SBTS.

Hoch-Smith, Judith
    1978   "Introduction." Pp. 1-23 in *Women in Ritual and Symbolic Roles.* Eds. Judith Hoch-Smith and Anita Spring. New York: Plenum.

Jackson, Rosemary
    1981   *Fantasy: The Literature of Subversion.* New York: Methuen.

Jameson, Fredric
    1981   *The Political Unconscious: Narrative as a Socially Symbolic Act.* Ithaca: Cornell University Press.
    1972   *The Prison-House of Language: A Critical Account of Structuralism and Russian Formalism.* Princeton: Princeton University Press.

Jay, Nancy
    1985   "Sacrifice as Remedy for Having Been Born of Woman." Pp. 283-309 in *Immaculate & Powerful: The Female in Sacred Image and Social Reality*. Boston: Beacon.

Kearney, Richard
    1988   *The Wake of Imagination: Toward a Postmodern Culture*. Minneapolis: University of Minnesota Press.

Ketterer, David
    1974   *New Worlds for Old: The Apocalyptic Imagination, Science Fiction and American Literature*. Bloomington: Indiana University Press.

Landy, Marcia
    1977   "The Silent Woman: Towards a Feminist Critique." Pp. 16-27 in *The Authority of Experience: Essays in Feminist Criticism*. Eds. Arlyn Diamond and Lee R. Edwards. Amherst: University of Massachusetts Press.

Lefanu, Sarah
    1988   *Feminism and Science Fiction*. Bloomington: Indiana University Press.

McGinn, Bernard
    1983   "Symbols of the Apocalypse in Medieval Culture." *Michigan Quarterly Review* 22:265-283.

Maclean, Marie
    1987   "Oppositional Practices in Women's Traditional Practices." *New Literary History* 19:37-50.

Moers, Ellen
    1978   *Literary Women*. London: The Women's Press.

Olsen, Lance
    1987   *Ellipse of Uncertainty: An Introduction to Postmodern Fantasy*. New York: Greenwood.

Palumbo, Donald
    1986   "Sexuality and the Allure of the Fantastic in Literature." Pp. 3-24 in *Erotic Universe: Sexuality and Fantastic Literature*. New York: Greenwood.

Propp, Vladimir
    1978   "Structure and History in the Study of the Fairy Tale." *Semeia* 10:57-83.

Rosinsky, Natalie M.
    1984   *Feminist Futures: Contemporary Women's Speculative Fiction*. Ann Arbor: UMI Research.

Rowe, Karen E.
    1979   "Feminism and Fairy Tales." *Women's Studies* 6:237-257.
    1986   "To Spin a Yarn: The Female Voice in Folklore and Fairy Tale." Pp. 53-74 in *Fairy Tales and Society: Illusion, Allusion, and Paradigm*. Philadelphia: University of Pennsylvania Press.

Russ, Joanna
    1972   "The Image of Women in Science Fiction." pp. 79–94 in *Images of Women in Fiction: Feminist Perspectives*. Ed. Susan Koppleman Cornillon. Bowling Green: Bowling Green State University Popular Press.

Scholes, Robert
    1981   "A Footnote to Russ's 'Recent Feminist Utopias.'" Pp. 86-87 in *Future Females: A Critical Anthology*. Ed. Marleen S. Barr. Bowling Green: Bowling Green State University Popular Press.

Spivak, Gayatri C.
    1983   "Displacement and the Discourse of Woman." Pp. 169-195 in *Displacement: Derrida and After*. Ed. Mark Krupnick. Bloomington: Indiana University Press.

Stone, Kay
    1986   "Feminist Approaches to the Interpretation of Fairy Tales." Pp. 229-235 in *Fairy Tales and Society*. Ed. Ruth Bottigheimer. Philadelphia: University of Pennsylvania Press.
    1985   "The Misuses of Enchantment." Pp. 125-145 in *Women's Folklore, Women's Culture*. Eds. Rosan Jordan and Susan Kalcik. Philadelphia: University of Pennsylvania Press.

Tatar, Maria
    1987   *The Hard Facts of the Grimms' Fairy Tales*. Princeton: Princeton University Press.

Tavis, Anna
    1986   "Fairy Tales from a Semiotic Perspective." Pp. 195-202 in *Fairy Tales and Society*. Ed. Ruth Bottigheimer. Philadelphia: University of Pennsylvania Press.

von Franz, Marie-Louise
    1972   *The Feminine in Fairytales*. Dallas: Spring.

Weber, Eugene
    1981   "Fairies and Hard Facts: The Reality of Folktales." *Journal of the History of Ideas* 42:93-113.

Yarbro Collins, Adela
    1987   "Women's History and the Book of Revelation." Pp. 80-91 in *SBL 1987 Seminar Papers*. Ed. Kent Richards. Atlanta: Scholars.
    1976   *The Combat Myth in the Book of Revelation*. Missoula: Scholars.

Zipes, Jack
    1986   "Marxists and the Illumination of Folk and Fairy Tales." Pp. 235-243 in *Fairy Tales and Society*. Ed. Ruth Bottigheimer. Philadelphia: University of Pennsylvania Press.

RESPONSE: FANTASY AND THE NEW TESTAMENT

Joanna Dewey
Episcopal Divinity School

1. *Introduction.*

It is my pleasure to respond to the two New Testament articles in this issue of *Semeia* on fantasy. As a specialist on Mark, well versed in literary and oral approaches to the gospels, and an active feminist critic, I come to these articles as an insider to the content and general approaches of the articles by George Aichele and Tina Pippin, but as an outsider to fantasy theory and its application to New Testament texts.

I began, as most of us do, with an intuitive sense of what fantasy in literature is. After reading Aichele's "The Fantastic in the Discourse of Jesus" and Pippin's "The Heroine and the Whore: Fantasy and the Female in the Apocalypse of John" and some of the introductory articles, I am less sure of what fantasy is in narrative. Perhaps this is a necessary first step in understanding fantasy. And in the process, I became convinced that fantasy is not the major tool for analysis used by either Aichele or Pippin.

Aichele demonstrates that Matthew and Luke remove some ambiguity and paradox from Mark—but is it the *fantastic* they are removing? Pippin's analysis of the Apocalypse shows that it is "a dangerous, unliberating text for women," but that seems to me to be due, not to "the fantastic representation of the female in the Apocalypse" (which is no more or less fantastic than the rest of the narrative) but to the gender code of the text. It is not "fantasy studies" that show the text to be unliberating for women but gender analysis. My conclusion, however, is not to discard fantasy theory for New Testament scholars. I think fantasy studies have inspired Aichele and Pippin to look at their texts in new and creative ways. Fantasy is part of our canonical texts, deserving of scholarly exploration.

2. *George Aichele: "The Fantastic in the Discourse of Jesus."*

Aichele has defined what he means by fantasy very precisely. He employs Todorov's understanding that the literary fantastic relates to the referential aspects of narrative in which it is unclear to the reader if the referent is to the marvelous—a supernatural world—or to the uncanny—strange events but with natural explanations. Fantasy then leaves the reader unclear or hesitant about its referents. Aichele considers it "inherently subversive of belief" since the reference system is unclear.

Since the gospels seem intended to promote belief, Aichele proposes to show how the later gospels, Matthew and Luke, de-fantasize fantastic elements in Mark and Thomas. He looks particularly at two dialogues (Mark 7:14-23 and par.; Mark 3:22-27 and par.), the identity of Jesus, and the synoptic apocalypse. His proposed method of approach seems sound enough, and his article does show Matthew and Luke to be clearer and less ambiguous than Mark. However, what he shows to be modified from Mark does not seem to me to fit his definition of the fantastic. Most of his discussion of his examples focuses on ambiguity and paradox in general, not on fantasy defined as hesitancy in reference between the marvelous and uncanny. Aichele appears to assume that ambiguity and paradox are fantastic. I do not believe this to be the case.

Before turning to the question, "Is what is deleted from Mark fantastic?" I want to make one further observation about Aichele's approach. He observes that the fantastic is intermittent in the canonical gospels, and that their larger narratives provide the "metatextual context within which the reader resolves indeterminacy of meaning. . . ." I do not believe Aichele applies this principle rigorously enough in his analysis. First he includes the gospel of Thomas along with Mark, even though, as he himself notes, it lacks narrative continuity and is quite "enigmatic." I believe its generic difference as a sayings collection rather than a narrative makes it confusing for comparison purposes, since its ambiguity may only be due to its lack of a narrative "metatextual context." Concatenations of sayings are bound to be more indeterminate than narrative.

Second, sometimes Aichele does not pay sufficient attention to the extent to which Mark's narrative may clarify apparent ambiguities. For example, regarding Mark 3:22-27 he asks, "Does the reader indeed know that Jesus' spirit is the Holy Spirit?" He notes that "holy" is not used to modify "spirit" in the baptism account in 1:10. However, the pericope immediately preceding the baptism ends "he will baptize you with the Holy Spirit" (1:8), so given the metatextual context, the reader is quite clear what spirit is descending upon Jesus.

Returning to the issue of whether or not what Aichele identifies as fantastic is fantastic, in the two dialogues Aichele selects as instances of Matthew and Luke deleting fantasy, he picks a core saying which he views as fantastic in which I fail to find the fantasy (Mark 7:15; Gos. Thom. 14; Mark 3:27). In the first instance, Aichele finds the fantastic particularly in the reference to "mouth" (Gos. Thom. 14). He sees the mouth as "uncanny and yet also marvelous," an "ambiguous place." Why? How is a mouth either marvelous or uncanny? The referent seems to me quite natural and obvious. Yes, the function of mouth as boundary may be disrupted, but does it thus become "paradoxical"? Similarly, Mark 7:15 is viewed as a "paradoxical saying" clarified by Mark's "quasi-scientific explanation" in vv. 18-23. Likewise, for Mark 3:22-27 Aichele sees the statement, "If Satan has risen up against himself and is divided, he cannot stand," as paradoxical.

I might question if these sayings actually qualify for the label "paradoxical." But more importantly, I want to make the point that paradox and fantasy are different generic forms. Aichele does not define paradox. The *Princeton Encyclopedia of Poetry and Poetics* defines paradox as, "A statement which seems untrue but proves valid upon close inspection" (598). M. H. Abrams considers paradox a form of "figurative language," "a statement that seems absurd or self-contradictory, but which turns out to have a tenable and coherent meaning" (36, 38). Paradox has to do with meaning or truth: the choice is either to accept the text's view of the paradoxical as true or to reject it as incoherent or gibberish. For fantasy, the tension has to do with choice between possible external referents. In the instance of Mark 7:14-23 and in most of the rest of Aichele's other examples from Mark, I believe he is discussing the issue of paradoxical meaning, not fantastic indeterminacy of referents. And these require quite different decisions on the part of the reader. For paradox, the reader is asked to accept some particular understanding or meaning or reject it as contradictory nonsense; for fantasy, the reader is left unable to decide between two possible systems of reference.

Again in his section on the identity of Jesus, Aichele appeals to paradox, in this case the passion rendering paradoxical Peter's identification of Jesus as the Messiah. And I would agree that Mark is presenting a paradoxical narrative: if the reader/hearer accepts Mark's narrative world view, this apparently abysmal failure, Jesus, really is the Son of God. Whether or not the reader understands the external referent for Son of God as supernatural or uncanny—and the metatextual context of Mark plus first–century world views suggest a supernatural understanding— the reader still perceives Mark's gospel as good news or rejects it as nonsense. The issue is not reference but acceptance or rejection of meaning. Paradox is again invoked in the discussion of the synoptic apocalypse, the paradox of "my words" and "this generation." Aichele concludes that it ends in "fantastic undecidability . . . for 'no one knows'" the time. Undecidable, yes, but how is this fantastic?

Aichele notes in his discussion that Mark and Thomas "announce their incompleteness, their own secrecy and the failure of that secrecy." In conclusion, he writes:

> We cannot dispense with the metaphysical security of a mythic enclosure—a self-consistent, complete, and therefore "real" world—no matter how illusory or totalitarian it may be. We require a hermeneutics to take otherwise meaningless objects or events and transform them into meaningful experience, a life, a story. That hermeneutics . . . is an incomplete and violent struggle for authority over a submissive yet resistant "text."

So far, I would agree with Aichele about the interpretation of narrative. He, however, sees the fantastic at the heart of this struggle: "The fantastic is the point at which that struggle is revealed for what it is." In this article, he has demonstrated to me that fantasy is not the locus of this struggle. In his earlier articles on the gospel traditions and the fantastic (see Aichele's note 1), he has indeed made a case for the existence of fantasy in these literatures. In this article, however, I believe Aichele is trying to make fantasy a more major key to the interpretation of narrative than it is. Paradox and ambiguity are not of themselves fantastic, and the resistance of narratives to conclusive interpretation goes far beyond either paradox or fantasy.

3. *Tina Pippin: "The Heroine and the Whore: Fantasy and the Female in the Apocalypse of John."*

Pippin basically assumes that the Apocalypse is a fantasy, one that subverts the political, economic and religious realities of the dominating power, while maintaining its "sexual oppression and stereotypes of woman as object of [male] violence and desire." Like Aichele, she uses Todorov's definition of the fantastic as falling between the marvelous (supernatural) and, for her, the mimetic (realistic). She uses Bakhtin's understanding of parody and the carnivalesque very effectively in her discussion of the brutal murder and dismemberment of the whore of Babylon. Pippin's primary interest, however, is not in showing how the Apocalypse is fantastic, but in investigating its gender code, in particular how the female is portrayed in this particular fantasy.

Pippin's article amply demonstrates her conclusion: "The misogyny which underlies this narrative is extreme." The implied author and implied reader/hearer of the Apocalypse (as of virtually all biblical narrative) are encoded in the narrative as male. And biblical scholars, women as well as men, are trained to read according to that code, as male. Judith Fetterley writes:

> the cultural reality is not the emasculation of men by women, but the *immasculation* of women by men. As readers and teachers and scholars, women are taught to think as men, to identify with a male point of view, and to accept as normal and legitimate a male system of values, one of whose central principles is misogyny. (xx)

Pippin has chosen *not* to follow the code inscribed in the text for the reader, but to read the text as a woman. Anyone pursuing this article on the female in the Apocalypse cannot help but notice the extent to which the female is "still marginalized, still banished to the edges of the text," still disempowered. A real strength of the article is how Pippin makes explicit the abundance of male sexual fantasy in the sexual imagery, seduction, and erotic tension of the narrative. The Apocalypse is unquestionably a "dangerous, unliberating text for women."

Pippin's article raises three questions for me. First, how is the misogyny of the Apocalypse related to fantasy? Second, is her interpretation of the gender code a bit too extreme? And third, can the Apocalypse be liberating for anyone, male or female? First, reading *any* androcentric text is likely to be unliberating for women. The problem with the Apocalypse for women is that it is androcentric and patriarchal, not that it is fantasy. Yet I think perhaps fantasy literature may be more destructive for women than realistic literature, because fantasy serves to heighten and exaggerate both the abhorrence of the female and the ideal of her passivity. Pippin writes: "The vision is real; the world of the unreal becomes real in fantasy literature," and, I would argue, thereby doubly dangerous.

Second, I do not believe the Apocalypse excludes all women from its vision of heaven. The expression, "144,000 men who have not defiled themselves with women" is, in my opinion, simply the author's androcentric mindset in operation. Nowhere else in early Christianity do we find women excluded. I doubt they are excluded here. If we could ask John of Patmos, I expect he would say of course women are included, though he might well subscribe to saying 114 in Thomas: "For every woman who makes herself a male will enter the Kingdom of heaven."

In addition, it presents the entire Christian community under the female image of the bride. Yet as Pippin writes, "The bride is woman as object, adorned and passive." Thus, in the fantasy of the Apocalypse not only are women disempowered and silent but so ultimately are men, as they are pictured under the image of the bride. Christian men are subsumed in passive female imagery.

This leads me to my final query: is the Apocalypse liberating even for men? Basically the function of the ideal Christian is to remain pure and to suffer until God's violence overthrows and destroys evil. David Barr writes of those who hear the Apocalypse read in worship:

> [They] live in a new reality in which lambs conquer and suffering rules. The victims have become the victors. They no longer suffer helplessly at the hands of Rome; they are now in charge of their own destiny and by their voluntary suffering they participate in the overthrow of evil and the establishment of God's kingdom. They now see themselves as *actors* in charge

> of their own destiny. And that is perhaps more of a victory than most folks achieved in first century Asia Minor. (50)

That may indeed have been more of a victory than most were able to achieve, but I believe it is a dangerous fantasy. It exalts voluntary suffering for everyone, regardless of class or gender, as a way to hasten God's violent retribution and to bring about the future blessed state. Such a world view exalts both passive suffering and violence. It is especially dangerous for women as victims of violence, but it is dangerous and unliberating for men as well, whether as the violent oppressor or the suffering oppressed. Misogyny is only one of the problems with the Apocalypse.

4. *Fantasy and the New Testament.*

In spite of my critiques of these two articles, I think fantasy theory provides a useful tool amid the various literary and psychological tools we bring to bear on our limited canon. I, too, would subscribe to some definition of literary fantasy as modifying one or more of the "ground rules" of consensual reality. However, beyond that I do not think focusing on the referents of the narrative is particularly helpful for New Testament texts, whether Aichele's distinction between the marvelous and the uncanny or Pippin's between the supernatural and the mimetic.

Concern for referents is characteristic of *print* media. Early Christians heard their texts; with few exceptions they did not read them. And hearing, especially in a group, is a present communal *experience* of the narrative world of the text, whether fantastic or "realistic." Issues of reference are not usually of major concern to listening audiences.

In addition, the notion from Todorov used by both Aichele and Pippin that in fantasy the reader must hesitate in her identification with the hero and "between a natural and a supernatural explanation of the events described" does not seem to me useful in regard to New Testament narratives. In both the synoptic gospels and the Apocalypse, the issue I find is not hesitation in regard to the external referents of the events described, but the call to accept the narrative "reality" presented as meaningful for one's life and community.

I find more useful than Todorov's the descriptions of fantasy by Rosemary Jackson and Jack Zipes. Jackson views (utopian) fantasy "as the potential for envisioning an 'other world,' a place or state of being which grants to those who can enter it the power to change the real world." Zipes says that fantasy "undermines reality and will not let us rest content with conditions as they are" and it "provides us with hope that the other . . . is possible." He writes, "The miraculous transformations in fairy tales reveal that life is a process of qualitative change in which the utopian element can emerge if people realize what their powers are." The idea of alternate realities empowering people to begin changing present realities makes sense in the oral/aural world of early Christians—one in which they experience the performance of a narrative, not seek out its external referents.

This sort of definition of fantasy seems to me a useful approach to New Testament narrative, and makes ethical issues central. Zipes concludes his article with the question: "Why do some works of fantasy nurture our imagination and bring about self-awareness while much of fantasy deludes us and reconciles us to the status quo?" In so far as the fantasy in the gospels or the Apocalypse empowers us to change ourselves and the real world, fantasy works for good; in so far as it reconciles us to long-suffering submission to a violent and oppressive status quo, fantasy promotes evil. Looking at fantasy in early Christian texts will help us to raise necessary ethical questions about our canonical literature.

WORKS CONSULTED

Abrams, M. H.
    1966   *A Glossary of Literary Terms*. New York: Holt, Rinehart and Winston.

Barr, David L.
    1984   "The Apocalypse as a Symbolic Transformation of the World: A Literary Analysis." *Interpretation* 38:39-50.

Fetterley, Judith
    1978   *The Resisting Reader: A Feminist Approach to American Fiction*. Bloomington: Indiana University Press.

Kermode, Frank
    1979   *The Genesis of Secrecy: On the Interpretation of Narrative*. Cambridge: Harvard University Press.

O'Connor, William Van
    1974   "Paradox." P. 598 in *Princeton Encyclopedia of Poetry and Poetics*. Ed. Alex Preminger. Enlarged Edition. Princeton: Princeton University Press.

THE BIBLE IN FANTASY

Colin Manlove
University of Edinburgh

ABSTRACT

The Bible has a special place in fantasy, because it is there alone of all literary forms that its supernatural events, divine personages, and miracles find their place. The Bible is not simply the truth: it is a fantastical truth. The first texts to rework it, however, biblical epics starting from the fourth century, treated it as the truth, and expanded but did not alter or reinterpret the original. One writer in this long tradition who did invent new scenes was Milton in *Paradise Lost* (1667), with possible loss of orthodoxy as a consequence. Christian fantasy really starts in the twelfth century with the Church sanction of the use of the marvelous to subserve Christian doctrine, and thus some license for the imagination. A basic technique in many of these Christian fantasies is to seem to "go away" from biblical narrative and doctrine in their strange worlds, and then come nearer through the surprise of what is scripturally there. Some, such as Marlowe's *Dr. Faustus* and Bunyan's *The Pilgrim's Progress*, enter into a peculiar dialogue with the Word. Dante's *Commedia* proves a Bible of the afterlife. But with Swedenborg and Blake, the Bible stories are either translated to concepts, or seen as products of the human imagination; Blake sets out to write a "Bible of Hell." The story after Blake is one of much more oblique or hidden use of the Bible, or simply less use of it, by writers of smaller stature. These post-Romantic fantasies are even more freely inventive than those before them, and to that extent more liable to lose touch with the Bible. Since C. S. Lewis, little more Christian fantasy has been written, and one finds science fiction writers using the Bible for more secular purposes.

---

1. *Introduction: The Bible as Fantasy.*

The Bible has a special place in fantasy, because it is there alone of all literary forms that its supernatural events, divine personages, and miracles find their place. The Christian religion—if such a thing may be spoken of any more, and with due respect to liberal or postmodernist theologians—is nothing apart from a few revolutionary *sententiae* without its supernatural base: even supposing we dismiss Genesis and Revelation as myths, if we do not predicate a God "out there" and a historical Christ somewhere, there is really not much left on which to found our faith except a sort of consecrated humanism. These points are made because it is possible for more sophisticated minds to see it as only too appropriate that the "magical" side of Christianity should find its literary home in fantasy. Without the "fantasy" in Christianity—and to that we shall return—the sayings of Jesus are at least as exciting as the invention of the wheel: but like the wheel they can do little else but go round and round on this earth. And yet it is the influence of the Bible as a secular conduct manual with God only as referee and heaven as the distant cup that has dominated Christain literature in the last two centuries, and to some extent prior to that. There are, in short, remarkably few Christian fantasies. And this despite the fact that the text and the history and the teleology on which Christianity is founded are pre-eminently of the mode of fantasy.

The Bible as fairy-tale or "fantasy": let us begin with that point. There are, of course, a good number of people prepared, despite all that has happened over the past two centuries, to believe every fantastic story in the Bible to be true: people still prepared to agree with the Reverend John William Burgon, who wrote in 1861:

> The BIBLE is none other than the *Voice of Him that sitteth upon the Throne!* Every book of it—every chapter of it—every word of it—every syllable of it—(where are we to stop?) every letter of it—is the direct utterance of the Most High! The Bible is none other than the word of God—not some part of it more, some part of it less, but all alike, the utterance of Him, who sitteth upon the Throne—absolute—faultless—unerring—supreme. (quoted in Landow:55)

But for those not quite prepared to be so literal, there is the possibility of saying that the Bible is a fantasy that is also a fact. An interesting case for this has been made by J. R. R. Tolkien in his essay "On Fairy Stories" (originally 1939), when he turns at the end to wonder whether fairy stories are at all founded on truth, and declares, "it has long been my feeling (a joyous feeling) that God redeemed the corrupt making-creatures, men, in a way fitting to this aspect, as to others, of their strange nature" (Tolkien:62). In other words, the Gospel story is one peculiar to our world, even while also being reality; God would choose other stories for the needs of different fallen creatures on other worlds, and thus what we have in the Bible is an image only as well as being truth, myth as well as fact. It is an idea that C. S. Lewis echoes in his own fantasies, where the story of man tempted, or of man's redemption, is different on the planet Perelandra or in the land of Narnia. If we put the point most starkly, what these writers do in their fantasies is write new "Bibles" for the needs of different worlds, from Malacandra to Middle-earth.

But Tolkien further assimilates the Bible of this world to the genre of fantasy:

> The Gospels contain a fairy-story, or a story of a larger kind which embraces all the essence of fairy-stories. They contain many marvels—peculiarly

artistic, beautiful, and moving: "mythical" in their perfect, self-contained significance; and among the marvels is the greatest and most complete conceivable eucatastrophe [the happy ending]. But this story has entered History and the primary world; the desire and aspiration of sub-creation has been raised to the fulfillment of Creation. (62-3)

Tolkien has several hierarchic categories of creation. Somewhere out beyond all knowing and imagery is the God who made all worlds; then there is that same God who created this world in a particular form requiring particular modes of divine act to sustain it, these acts being enshrined in a highly individual text we call the Bible—which whether or not immediately God's word, does give the form of God's acts. Then there are the mortal rational creatures peculiar to this word, some of them writers, some of them writers of fantasy drawing directly or indirectly on the narrative rhythms and "myths" of the Bible; and no doubt beneath these are the wish-fulfillers, the self-deceivers, the liars and the cheats. Thus it may be said that the writer of fantasy partakes in the narrative of the Bible, because both belong to the same mode: and thus that, albeit in a broken and clouded sense, such writers are themselves creating bibles.

> The Evangelium has not abrogated legends; it has hallowed them, especially the "happy ending." The Christian has still to work, with mind as well as body, to suffer, hope and die; but he may now perceive that all his bents and faculties have a purpose, which can be redeemed. So great is the bounty with which he has been treated that he may now, perhaps, fairly dare to guess that in Fantasy he may actually assist in the effoliation and multiple enrichment of creation. All tales may come true; and yet, at the last, redeemed, they may be as like and as unlike the forms that we give them as Man, finally redeemed, will be like and unlike the fallen that we know. (63)

Now whether or not we agree with Tolkien, it is certainly the case that Christian fantasy, in however peculiar a mode it may be framed, does partake in certain of the basic narratives and rhythms of the Bible. (Of course, many "pagan" myths have similar rhythms, such as the Demeter/Persephone, or the Cupid and Psyche stories, or even the felt imminence of "good news" or "gospel" in Virgil's *Fourth Eclogue*: but C. S. Lewis would argue that it is possible to participate in Bible events both before and after the fact [Lewis, 1958], and indeed wrote his version of the "pagan" Cupid and Psyche myth, *Till We Have Faces* [1956], partly to show this.)

We have, for example, in George MacDonald's *Phantastes* (1858), the story of a young man who enters Fairy Land, something of a picture of innocence, fall, and redemption: the hero Anodos disobeys a specific prohibition and acquires a shadow which poisons all that he sees; he loses the shadow only when he learns how to lose his self; his last act in Fairy Land is a Christ-like one of sacrifice for others. Or in MacDonald's late fantasy, *Lilith*, we have something of a vision of the Last Things. In Charles Kingsley's *The Water-Babies* (1863), we might think, as Kingsley jokingly teases us, that "this is a fairy tale, and all fun and pretence; and . . . you are not to believe one word of it, even if it is true" (Kingsley, 1863:86); we might believe that we are simply dealing with a whimsically-created marine creature traveling a stream in Victorian Yorkshire and then touring river, sea, and ocean: but under the narrative is a pattern of development of a heathen soul through baptism to a spiritual law lived first under law and eventually through grace—in short, a development from the vicissitudes of the Hebrew Bible to the divine gifts of the New Testament.

2. *The Emergence of Christian Fantasy.*

This partaking in the truth of the Bible is more and less direct. There is for instance a long tradition of biblical epic, from Gaius Juvencus's *Evangeliorum libri quatuor* of c. 330 CE to Friedrich Klopstock's *Messias* (1751-73), where materials of the Bible are expanded and dramatized without at all conflicting with or adding to the whole (Kirkconnell, 1952 and 1973; Lewalski:37-101). Du Bartas' *La Sepmaine* (1578), for example, is an enormous expansion of the few verses in Genesis 1 describing the creation; Valvasone's *L'Angeleida* (1590) dilates on the brief mention of a war in heaven in Revelation 12:7-9; and Hugo van Grotius' *Adamus Exul* (1601) devotes five acts and 2042 lines to the few verses in Genesis describing the fall. Many of such works are written in the period 1500-1700 when the expansive and exploratory Renaissance spirit was at its height, and their great culmination is in that extraordinarily ambitious poem *Paradise Lost*. The aim is the paradoxical one of enlarging on the biblical account while remaining within its essential confines. As example consider the early version of the creation of man, by Avitus in his *Poematum de Mosaicae Historiae Gestis* (507 CE). The Bible has, "So God created man in his own image," and, a second time, "And the Lord God formed man of the dust of the ground, and breathed into his nostrils the breath of life; and man became a living soul" (Gen 1:27; 2:7). Avitus devotes almost sixty lines to the subject, which he considers both from the point of view of the shaping hand of an artist with clay, and from that of an anatomist in reverse:

> Stiff with knobs,
> The spine in close communication spreads
> A double wickerwork of ordered ribs.
> The inward parts are framed for life's new uses;
> A natural shelter for the heart is made,
> Whose hanging mass amid the crowded vitals

Is hidden deep. The lung is added, too,
Which feeds upon thin air, when, being given
Nostrils of gentle breathing, it takes in
And renders back again the atmosphere,
And then once more new inhalation knows.
The right side of the liver holds a fountain
That must with blood be quickened; thence the veins
Spread a blind river through the viscera.
To the left part, the spleen's rule is assigned,
By which, they say, the hair and cut nails grow.
These in the living body have their source,
Yet when they are cut off, they feel no pain;
From the spleen's power they renew their growth. . . .

(Book I, 99-113; trans. Kirkconnell, 1952:4-5)

Despite some broad indebtedness to such accounts of creation as those in Lucretius' *De Rerum Natura* (Books III-V) or Ovid's *Metamorphoses* (Book I) the picture here is one of remarkable scientific curiosity—anticipating that sense of God's sophisticated workmanship behind the amazing design of the natural world which appears again in eighteenth-century deism and in nineteenth-century "natural theology" (as inspired by Paley and Whewell). But for all this originality, Avitus in no way fundamentally alters the biblical account: what he provides amounts to an explanatory gloss, or, to use another analogy, a view through a microscope and with slowed camera speed of what in the Bible is over as a total process within a few general words. His daring, as of all hexaemeral and other writers of biblical epic is in grafting on to the original a classical mode which virtually transforms its genre: and to this, like most early patristic poets, he was keenly sensitive (Lewalski:42-3).

However, the primary biblical events focused on by these re-workings are the more "cosmic" ones—the creation, the war in heaven, the temptation and fall of man, the passion of Christ and His redemption of the world, the biblical sources for which, apart from the last, are more or less over within the first three chapters of Genesis (Kirkconnell, 1973:315-21). There is little extant literary reworking of the stories of Moses or of Abraham, not least perhaps because the biblical account of them is already very detailed. The interest in the large and supernaturally ultimate elements of the biblical story shown by these works makes them naturally look to the epic as the genre best suited to express them: but what must concern us is that the interest itself in these matters, however based on a desire to provide a total Christian explanation of the universe, springs from and appeals to that potentially theologically dangerous faculty, the imagination.

The point at which the imagination takes off is not always easy to quantify. Does it come where there is a re-interpretation of the official account, as in certain Gnostic and rabbinical versions of the temptation in Eden, where Satan is described as having physically seduced Eve (Evans:33, 46-8, 55; *Jewish Encyclopaedia*, s.v. "Eve," "Lilith"; Lacarrière:81-2)? Is it present in the invention of a range of characters to oppose heaven and inhabit hell, from Satan to Beelzebub, Mammon, or Belial, as in Joost van den Vondel's *Lucifer* (1654)? More evidently of course it comes where there is addition of wholly new episodes to the account, such as the transformation in hell of the devils to serpents in *Paradise Lost*: or more striking still in that poem, the elaborately-described journey of Satan out of hell through chaos towards the newly-created world.

Of all biblical epics *Paradise Lost* alone seems to deserve the title of a "fantasy," for here Milton has let his imagination loose among immensity as none before him. If in most official details the poem may be said to conform to the possibilities of the biblical account, in character and imagery it gives us virtually a new cosmos. The orientation of the Bible is primarily towards humans and their relations with God: the "celestial cycle" of war in heaven, creation and the nature of hell do not preoccupy it—with the possible exception of Revelation, which is still concerned with humanity's experience of the last days. More even than any of his predecessors in biblical epic, Milton has brought those great matters to the center of his poem, so that we wonder at the colossal, tortured geography of hell, the huge door out of it into the vast atmospheric turmoil of chaos, and then the journey towards light, the vision of the translucent heavens spreading continentally into all distance, and beneath them, suspended by a golden chain, the little Ptolemaic universe of concentric spheres, at the heart of which turns the earth and with it man still innocent.

Behind the sweep of Milton's verse and the spread of the landscapes of the poem—themselves quite new in the relatively unpictured cosmoses of previous epics—we sense an impulse which in contrast to his forbears is not more doctrinal than it is imaginative. And therein, as said before, lies danger. For when the imagination is given so long a lead, the visions with which it returns may no longer fit comfortably with what might be implied by or deduced from the biblical account. That is, in fact, what I have elsewhere argued happens in *Paradise Lost*, where the large scale "archetypal" imagery of the poem is that of a mandala, and suggests through this and other elements that rather than being the enemy to be rejected, Satan as serpent is the final element necessary to the balance and health of the universe (Manlove, 1978 and 1992).

Already we are breaking out of biblical epic and into the realm of "fantasy." Compared to biblical epic there are very few Christian fantasies, and yet they number some of the finest works of literature we have—the French *Queste del Saint Graal* (1215-30), Dante's *La Commedia* (1307-21), the Middle English *Pearl* (1375-95), Book I of Spenser's *The Faerie Queene* (1589), Marlowe's *Dr. Faustus* (1604), Milton's *Paradise Lost* (1667) and Bunyan's *The Pilgrim's Progress* (1678). All apart from Milton have a much more indirect relation to the Bible. Dante could be said to have written something like a Bible of the afterlife. His poem is of course scattered with biblical references, with special foci as we approach Beatrice at the close of the *Purgatorio* and the hosts surrounding the celestial rose at the end of the *Paradiso*. But here Dante is concerned to teach not by instructions from within this world, but through monitions and promises transmitted from those further worlds which form humanity's final lot. Of course, those worlds as presented in the poem can only be images. And yet it is typical of Dante at his time to claim that those images are not self-begotten but given.

The basic idea of the *Commedia*, the vision of the after-life of hell and heaven, had a long tradition behind it; and like Dante all the authors of such works claimed that they had been given to them on divine authority: but Dante clearly goes far beyond his predecessors both in invention and in elaboration of doctrine (Manlove,1992:22, 307n.6). To repeat, his aim could be said to have created a Bible of the after-life; perhaps even to have inverted the man-oriented Scripture that we have to a devil and god-oriented one (certainly images of inversion, in the form of funnels going down, then up and then out, are behind the three books). How better to teach man the price of his sin or the reward of his goodness should he ignore or follow the injunctions of the earthly Bible? And we may, if we will, find a closer rhythmic bond between our Bible and Dante's story, which in the *Inferno* describes a fall into deeper and deeper sin, in the *Purgatorio* a spiritual life lived under first law and then grace, and in the *Paradiso* the ascension of the redeemed soul to the heights of bliss: in short a history parallel to that recounted in the Old and New Testaments. But the poem is still more Christian than it is biblical in its account of how sin enslaves and binds us, and how the grace of Christ alone can make us truly pursue that upward journey which is permitted Dante only under temporary dispensation.

3. *The Two Texts of Fantasy and Scripture.*

Of its very nature, since it could be described as "a fiction involving the Christian supernatural, in an imagined world," Christian fantasy is born in *opposition* to the tradition of biblical re-telling. What fantasy may do is produce an alternative picture to convey biblical truths. That of course implies allegory or symbolism, and in fact the imagination is much freer than that. So from the start fantasy must appear to *go away* from Christianity to come nearer. Thus in *Pearl* we may think that the meeting between the dreamer and the pearl-covered girl is only secular, and indeed that in some mortal sense he is recovering a pearl that he has lost, until she turns to tell him that she is not his any more for she is a risen soul through the grace of Christ. And furthermore we may think that we are reading a "mere" fiction until that fiction begins to found itself in the Bible. The girl speaks of herself as having been made a queen in heaven, and justifies her apparently unmerited elevation by citing the parable of the vineyard in Matthew 20:1-16, whereby those who came late in the day to work in a householder's vineyard were paid the same as those who had worked all day (*Pearl*, sect. 9). Analogy with the Bible then becomes literal as towards the end of the poem the dreamer is granted a vision of the City of God as described in Revelation 21. Here, then, apparently free and secular fiction becomes caught up in the larger web of spiritual truth, and the Bible becomes the "subtextual" fact of the whole fable.

One might observe a similar process at work in the French *Queste del Saint Graal*, which describes the search by knights of King Arthur's Round Table for the Holy Grail. It seems purely a competitive adventure, although increasingly we are made aware that success in knightly contests is dependent not on physical prowess but on moral and bodily chastity. For long we are not to know that the Grail is any more than the magical object of legend that it was in the sources, particularly in Chrétien de Troyes. The author of the *Queste* may seem to have exploited the recent ecclesiastical liberality concerning the use of the marvelous, hitherto proscribed as heathen, in literature (Le Goff:28-9, 32). But that is because he has done as the Church intended, that is, used the Arthurian and supernatural elements to subserve a Christian and scriptural purpose (Manlove, 1992:12-20). Gloss after gloss is put on every event and object in the *Queste* to bring it within the borders of Christian and biblical teaching. Once again we "go away" into the fiction to be surprised back again. The whole story is shot through with language of desire drawn on the Song of Songs, and there is frequent veiled reference to 1 Corinthians 2 on the transmortal character of experience of God; the scriptural theme of the covenant between God and man described in the Pentateuch underscores the entire *Queste*; and there is not a moment without some passing hermit or wise man explaining his latest adventure to a knight in terms of divine reality:

> "The lady whom you saw astride the serpent, she is the Synagogue, the first Law, that was put aside as Jesus Christ had introduced the New. The serpent that carries her denotes the Scripture wrongly understood and misconstrued; it is hypocrisy and heresy, iniquity and mortal sin, it is the enemy himself: the serpent who through pride was hurled from paradise, the same which said to

Adam and his wife: 'If you eat this fruit you shall be like God,' and by this saying implanted the seed of concupiscence in their hearts." (122-3)

The adventure, the *fictum*, is allowed momentarily to be itself before it is caught up in a larger pattern and a greater text; just as apparently local and worldly acts have to relinquish their autonomy.[1]

The Bible has a special role as revealed Word in certain post-Reformation Christian fantasies. In Marlowe's *Dr. Faustus*, we find the good doctor perverting the express words of the Bible from the start, as he reviews all branches of learning before "settling" (as though it were not pre-decided) for necromancy.

> *Jeromes* Bible *Faustus*, view it well:
> *Stipendium peccati mors est*: ha, *Stipendium*, &c.
> The reward of sin is death? that's hard:
> *Si pecasse negamus, fallimur, et nulla est in nobis veritas*: If we say that we have no sinne we deceive our selves, and there is no truth in us.
> Why then belike
> We must sinne, and so consequently die,
> I, we must die, an everlasting death.
> What doctrine call you this? *Che sera, sera*:
> What will be, shall be; *Divinitie* adeiw. (I.i.73-83)

What Faustus does here is omit the clauses of saving grace through Jesus Christ that follow both statements: "but the gift of God is eternal life through Jesus Christ our Lord" (Romans 6:23); "If we confess our sins, he is faithful and just to forgive us our sins, and to cleanse us from all unrighteousness" (1 John 1:9). Faustus ignores these verses deliberately (we have just been told that he is an expert in theology) so that he can falsely indict divinity before moving on to necromancy. But that severance of himself from truth is directly paralleled by his giving his soul into the hands of a liar, the devil. The play then becomes a drama of different kinds of "word." There are the words of Faustus' spells as magician; there are the words of his bond in blood with the devils; and beyond that there is the revealed Word of a far greater magician than he. That larger Word writes itself on the play in the way that the words "despair" and "hell," which Faustus at first treats so casually as he does, come to have a terrible meaning for him when he no longer has the will to do anything about them. We may also see the play as a larger enactment of the two pieces of Scripture already quoted: Faustus is a sinner, and because he ignores the saving grace of Christ he suffers what he rewrote as the reward of sin, namely everlasting death. Nowhere is that Scripture more terribly written than in the last scene of the play, where Faustus waits in horror for the devils to seize him and testifies only to the paralysis of his soul as he struggles in vain towards the redemptive blood of Christ streaming above him in the firmament: "One drop would save my soule, halfe a drop, ah my Christ."

We find Scripture playing a large part in Christian fantasy again in Bunyan's *The Pilgrim's Progress* (1678), where Christian's journey is initiated by his reading in a book that fills him with terror at its dire warning of the destruction to befall his city. He sets out with the book in his hand, and still has it after he has got through the Slough of Despond, fallen victim to Mr. Worldly Wiseman and been put back in the right way by Mr. Evangelist. We hear no more of the book, only of how Christian loses the burden on his back and is given a roll to carry. We must suppose that after he has entered the Wicket-Gate, Christian has as it were "entered" the book, and started to live the spiritual life that it describes: and certainly the continual citation of biblical texts in the margins of the text gives some emblematic impression of his living within a spiritual body. And the peculiar insistence of Bunyan's pilgrimage story on the need to keep to the one path (Manlove, 1992:118-22) can be seen as a form of the Puritan keeping to the single and clear sense of Scripture as the way towards heaven. Even at the end, when Christian is sinking in the last river, Hopeful declares, "My Brother, you have quite forgot the Text . . ." (Bunyan, 1954: 157).

Still more striking, and even grotesque, treatment of the Bible in what may be called a Christian fantasy can be seen in Bunyan's other great theological drama, his spiritual autobiography, *Grace Abounding to the Chief of Sinners* (1666). In this text the Word assumes so great a reality that it becomes an active agent in the story, as Bunyan struggles in his spirit to find a text in Scripture that will satisfactorily answer another that terrifies him. The bugbear concerns Esau's selling of his birthright, which Bunyan identifies with his own treatment of Christ, "For ye know how that afterward, when he would have inherited the blessing, he was rejected: for he found no place of repentance, though he sought it carefully with tears" (Heb 12:17). The resolution to this occurs after Bunyan has discovered a comforting text ("My grace is sufficient unto thee" [2 Cor 12:9]) and then hopes to be able to set the two texts at one another like dogs in his head: "Well, about two or three days after, so they did indeed; they bolted both upon me at a time, and did work and struggle strangely in me for a while; at last, that about Esau's birthright began to wax weak, and withdraw, and vanish; and this about the sufficiency of grace prevailed with peace and joy" (1928:66-67). In Bunyan's mind a text has the solidity, and more, of a physical event, "These words were to my soul like fetters of brass to my legs" (1928:44); "this sentence stood like a mill-post at my back" (1928:60); "And truly I did now feel myself to sink into a gulf, as an house whose foundation is destroyed" (1928:62). For a Puritan who believed in the central importance of the Word, and that Scripture is the immediate voice of God, the Bible could have an all too terrible immediacy.

In Spenser's *Faerie Queene*, Book I, "The Legend of Holiness," we find Scripture playing another role. The first monster that the hero Redcrosse has to overthrow is Error, who vomits in her death a mass of books and pamphlets. Defeat certain textual errors though he may, the Redcrosse knight for long wanders, subject to delusions engineered by devilish agents. But Fairy Land represents in one way the landscape of his own soul, and what he meets in part depends on the quality of his spiritual sight. It is only when he has, through grace, been able to penetrate the phantoms that seek to deceive and detain him, that he breaks through the shows of the poisoned individual imagination and comes upon images which are domiciled in Scripture: Duessa becomes the Whore of Babylon astride the monster in Revelation 17, the last dragon which Redcrosse must slay in a form of the devil who will be cast down at the Last Judgment (Rev 20), and the rescued parents of Una, companion of Redcrosse, figure Adam and Eve freed by a figure of Christ from bondage to sin. In short, the procedure is a movement through a series of false texts to a true one, and from the imagination as perverse illusion to that imagination which expresses divine truth (compare Kane).

4. *The End of Christian Fantasy.*

But in the eighteenth century the Bible began to lose some of its credibility, began to be seen as a collection of mythic versions of truth. With Swedenborg's *Heaven and Hell* (1758), we have a work in which the notion of a Christian narrative has disappeared: there is no fall of man, no redemption in Christ and no Last Judgment. Swedenborg sees man as simply choosing between two tendencies, one heavenly, the other hellish, within him: the implication is almost one of a scientific pull of forces, and indeed Swedenborg was for a time, before the mystic visions that gave him his *Heaven and Hell*, a famous applied physicist. To read the Bible aright, it cannot be taken literally, but must be read, like every object in nature, in a hidden spiritual sense, because in Swedenborg's view all matter, whether in physical or written form, is the expression of a spiritual reality. Thus, the physical sun is an analogue of the heavenly one; thus too the New Jerusalem described in Revelation 21 is neither literal nor part of any Last Judgment to come, but rather serves to emblematize spiritual truths which the angels perceive substantially:

> By the new heaven and new earth they understand a new Church. By the city Jerusalem coming down from God out of heaven, they understand its heavenly doctrine revealed by the Lord. By its length, breadth and height which

are equal and each twelve thousand furlongs, they understand all the various forms of good and truth contained in that doctrine taken collectively. By the wall of the city they understand the truths which protect it.... (No.307)

In this way the mythic content of the Bible is evacuated. Despite the appearances involved in so transforming vivid particulars to colorless concepts, it was Swedenborg's belief that spiritual things were far more substantial than the material objects and symbols we find so immediate.

Blake continues Swedenborg in reading the Bible in a spiritual sense. But where Swedenborg could still see the Bible as the secret code of a real heaven, Blake considers heaven and hell, God and devil, as parts of the human mind. For Blake the Bible is one more myth of a spiritual rhythm of fall and recovery present in all human experience. Blake objects to the tyranny which has made an objective, jealous God, and a "real" heaven and hell to confine and terrorize man. He writes his *The Marriage of Heaven and Hell* (1790) to unseat the Bible as a set text, and the objectivity of the Christian supernatural scheme and "Christian" codes of conduct. He does so by rewriting the Bible from the Devil's point of view, to create another and alternative myth at war with that disseminated by the followers of God. In a sense he uses Swedenborg as his opponent in the poem because where Swedenborg wrote what was substantially a bible of heaven (hell has small space in his account), Blake's object is to write its opposite: "I have also The Bible of Hell, which the world shall have whether they will or no" (191). The world never did have this bible, but in *The Marriage*, Blake certainly showed the way to the formerly orthodox angel he brought to his way of thinking: "This Angel, who is now become a Devil, is my particular friend; we often read the Bible together in its infernal or diabolical sense, which the world shall have if they behave well" (191).

For Blake the text of the Bible is no more fixed than the events it describes: the process of reading as of living must be a continual revolution, a dislocation of previous assumptions. (Blake seems here almost to anticipate the postmoderns.) So in his "Christian fantasy," *The Marriage of Heaven and Hell*, "Christian" turns out to be constantly other than we suppose; the poem is part fiction, part direct and overt statement; its mode shifts between poetry and prose; and we are continually pulled between our allegiance to its revolutionary statements and our awareness that they emerge from a biased individual, here the "devil." The whole poem is an emblematic refusal of the "set text" aspect that the Bible has hitherto possessed: it demonstrates by its own existence the folly of freezing literature to fixed and thereby tyrannous meaning; and by its ceaseless dialectic it refuses the simple God's-eye view of correct moral behavior that Blake finds in the Bible. This approach to the Bible as "set text" is behind the account of infernal printing:

> I was in a Printing house in Hell, & saw the method in which knowledge is transmitted from generation to generation.
>
> In the first chamber was a Dragon-Man, clearing away the rubbish from a cave's mouth; within, a number of Dragons were hollowing the cave.
>
> In the second chamber was a Viper folding round the rock & the cave, and others adorning it with gold, silver and precious stones.
>
> In the third chamber was an Eagle with wings and feathers of air: he caused the inside of the cave to be infinite; around were numbers of Eagle-like men who built palaces in the immense cliffs.
>
> In the fourth chamber were Lions of flaming fire, raging around & melting the metals into living fluids.
>
> In the fifth chamber were Unnam'd forms, which cast the metals into the expanse.
>
> There they were reciev'd by Men who occupied the sixth chamber, and took the forms of books & were arranged in libraries. (187)

The end point of the process in that deadening last sentence is clearly for Blake inadequate. The energies only "took the forms of books": we are to get beyond the apparently inert product to the whole dynamic process behind its creation. To read aright is to be aware of the text as part of a living sequence. That is one reason for Blake's saying that he will print "in the infernal method, by corrosives, which in Hell are salutary and medicinal, melting apparent surfaces away, and displaying the infinite which was hid" (187).[2] And that is what he has done here with the Bible.

Blake is a symptom, not a cause, of the marginalization of the Bible in fantasy and indeed any literature since his time. One need not cite the mythographers, the liberal theologians or the impact of Darwin as causes, nor rehearse at length the effects, in the removal of Christianity as the central intellectual fabric of society, and in the paucity of literary works expressing it. Christian fantasy had long since lost the high literary status it had in a more religious age, and was now written by relatively minor and marginal figures (Manlove, 1992: 156-8). In place of the Bible, the book of God, we now find much more emphasis on the book of nature as a text to be read to decipher the divine presence. Indeed, it is fair to say that Christian fantasy now becomes more apologetic in character, attempting to show through fiction the immanent presence of God within a world that now seemed more divorced from God (Manlove, 1992:158-60). "I have tried," wrote Charles Kingsley of his *The Water-Babies* (1863), "to make children and grown folks understand that there is a quite miraculous and divine element underlying all physical nature" (Kingsley, 1876, 2:137): and whether "underlying," or "on top of," or "throughout," the existence of the divine in the apparently physical world is the central topic in the fantasies of George MacDonald, Charles Williams, and C. S. Lewis.

5. Conclusion: Modern Fantasy.

As said, Christian fantasy owes its very existence from the first to the way that it goes apparently away from the Bible to produce Christian truths through new images. But the distance between modern Christian fantasy and the Bible is still greater. It is seen analogously in the way that in an earlier age such fantasies make clear their sources and the larger "set text" in which they are to be viewed: the apparently knightly virtues required to gain sight of the Grail are continually shown as Christian ones, the girl in *Pearl* identifies herself as one of the blessed in the scriptural heaven, and the names Redcrosse or Christian are sufficiently indicative of the frame in which we should read.

But in modern fantasy we have few such ready identifications: it is for us to translate Tom's journey in *The Water-Babies*, or the wandering adventures of MacDonald's Anodos in his *Phantastes* (1858); for us, too, to see what we will in such names as Anodos, Aslan, or Maleldil. It takes a fairly sharp reader to see that in MacDonald's *At the Back of the North Wind* (1871), Diamond's mystic experiences with North Wind look back to the visions in Ezekiel or in Daniel 10. A feature of modern Christian fantasies is that they are much more invented, much less founded on previous textual models, as the *Queste* looks to Chrétien or Wolfram's *Parzival*, the *Commedia* or *Pearl* to the tradition of visions of the other world, Spenser to Ariosto and Tasso, Marlowe to the *Faustbook*, *The Pilgrim's Progress* to the literature of spiritual pilgrimage. The imagination, no longer bounded by doctrine, is given freer rein to invent.

The result, in the end, can be the heterocosm, whereby an entirely new world is created with its own manifestations of spiritual truth, which cannot be reduced to our terms. Of this, as said, a good instance is C. S. Lewis's *The Lion, the Witch and the Wardrobe* (1950), the first book of his *Chronicles of Narnia*. Aslan the lion, though he carries out a Christ-like act of self-sacrifice and rises again, does it to save just one individual, Edmund, not the whole of Narnian kind. The rhythm of his act is like the story in the Gospels, but it is the idiom of God in this particular created world. Here a lion, however much he may be related to Christ the Lion of Judah in Revelation 5:5, is so in part because Narnia is a land of Talking Beasts. Or again, in Lewis's *Perelandra* (1943), where a story of a temptation and averted fall develops on the planet Venus mythically conceived, the protagonist Ransom is brought to realize that he cannot make analogies with or argue from the situation as it "was" on Earth, in Eden, because each story is wholly new: "nothing was a copy or model of anything else" (165). (It is remarkable how often modern writers of fantasy reject the idea of allegory in their work.) Ransom is led to express this point in terms of texts also: "This chapter, this page, this very sentence, in the cosmic story was utterly and eternally itself; no other passage that had occurred or ever would occur could be substituted for it" (166).

The point seems to hold, strangely enough, even in certain Christian fantasies set in our world—those of that bizarre theological mind, Charles Williams. It is of note that modern Christian fantasists are usually in some way heterodox or outré in their beliefs. Williams had the belief that the acts of Christ were eternally co-present: or, to put it another way, that in God there is no time, and thus what Adam did in Eden in naming the beasts may be recapitulated in an English village of the 1920s (Williams, 1931); or that Christ's suffering is continually active, and that it is possible through the loving exchange that that suffering represents, for someone in the twentieth century to remove from an ancestor in the fifteenth the terror felt at approaching death at the stake (Williams, 1945). Even while Williams writes within the context and the parameters of the Christian message as it was incarnated on earth, his theology is so individual as at least to transform, if not fly free from, our understanding of scriptural events.

There remain, as hinted, certain rhythms native to the Bible story which repeat themselves in modern Christian fantasy—creation, innocence, fall, life under law, redemption, life under grace, final judgment. But we should be careful not too rigorously to apply patterns which may in analogous forms be found in what Northrop Frye has called "secular scripture." We can, as seen, for instance, predicate a total Christian history from creation through fall, redemption, and ultimate apocalypse in George MacDonald's *Phantastes* and *Lilith* taken together; but we could as readily see the movement between the two in Jungian terms, with escape from the mother and rebirth in the one followed by return to her in the other.

Thereafter we are with those writers of fantasy—or even of science fiction—who have moved away from not only the Bible but Christianity itself into, most commonly, Gnosticism, but also Sufism, Zoroastrianism, Judaism, or Buddhism. Among Gnostic writers we might number David Lindsay, Mikhail Bulgakov, or Philip K. Dick. We have a new Bible of the Uttermost West given to the Mormons. We have stories which draw on biblical imagery but in which the Christian element has been transformed or re-interpreted, as in, say, Michael Moorcock's *Behold the Man* (1969), where Christ is seen as a bungling time-traveler from the present day; or in Doris Lessing's *Shikasta* (1979), in which the stories in the Bible are seen as misunderstandings of the creation of life on Earth by benign extraterrestrials whose schemes went wrong; or in Russell Hoban's *Riddley Walker* (1980), where the myths and cadences of the Bible are present to gloss the chaos and cultural incoherence of a post-holocaust society. In these and other works, the Bible and Christianity are still present as implicit comparators, but are melting into a sea of metaphysics where no belief system remains.

This, at least, at the level of literature as we presently have it. Whether, given the now diminished strength of the Christian faith, the Bible might ever return as a set text, seems a possibility at best to play with. There could be some fundamentalist victory leading to a new theocracy: it is a hypothesis explored by several science fiction writers, including Philip K. Dick in his *The Divine Invasion* (1981). But at present it is not visible. What is much more visible is the disappearance of the printed word altogether, and with it of the habit of reading itself. In that event the continuance of any kind of set text would be endangered past recall.

NOTES

1. Compare the near-contemporary remarks of Bernardus Silvestris, author of the no-less marvelous *Cosmographia* (c. 1150), when discussing what he calls the "integument" of Virgil's *Aeneid*, "The integument is a type of exposition which wraps the apprehension of truth in a fictional narrative, and thus it is also called an *involucrum*, a cover" (Sylvestris, 1979:5). This makes the invention, the "*fictum*," wholly subserve meaning or allegory.

2. And this of course is exactly what Blake did by his own method of etching his works on copperplate, as with *The Marriage of Heaven and Hell* itself.

WORKS CONSULTED

Anonymous
    1958   *Pearl*. Ed. E. V. Gordon. London: Oxford University Press.
    1969   *La Queste del Saint Graal*. Trans. and ed. Pauline Matarasso as *The Quest of the Holy Grail*. Harmondsworth: Penguin.

Ariosto, Ludovico
    1516   *Orlando Furioso*. Trans. Barbara Reynolds. 2 vols. Harmondsworth: Penguin, 1973, 1977.

Avitus, Alcimus Edicius
    1952   *Poematum de Mosaicae Historiae Gestis Libri quinque*. Pp. 325-82 in J. P. Migne, *Patrologia Latina* 59 (1862). Translated sections in Kirkconnell, 1952:3-19.

Bernardus Silvestris
    1973   *The Cosmographia of Bernardus Silvestris*. Trans. and intro. Winthrop Wetherbee. New York and London: Columbia University Press.

Blake, William
- 1961 *The Marriage of Heaven and Hell.* In *William Blake: His Complete Poetry and Prose.* Ed. Geoffrey Keynes. London: Nonesuch.

Bulgakov, Mikhail
- 1967 *The Master and Margarita.* Trans. Michael Glenny. London and New York: Harvill and Harper & Row.

Bunyan, John
- 1928 *Grace Abounding to the Chief of Sinners.* In *Grace Abounding and the Life and Death of Mr. Badman.* London: J. M. Dent.
- 1954 *The Pilgrim's Progress.* London: J. M. Dent.

Chrétien de Troyes
- 1982 *Le Conte du Graal.* Trans. Nigel Bryant as *Perceval: The Story of the Grail.* Arthurian Studies V. Woodbridge, Suffolk, and Totowa: D. S. Brewer and Rowman and Littlefield.

Dante Alighieri
- 1970-75 *La Divina Comedia.* Trans and ed. Charles S. Singleton as *The Divine Comedy.* 3 vols. Bollingen Series LXXX. Princeton: Princeton University Press.

Dick, Philip K.
- 1981 *The Divine Invasion.* New York: Timescape.

Du Bartas, Guillaume de Saluste, Sieur
- 1979 *La Sepmaine.* Trans. Joshuah Sylvester and ed. Susan Snyder in *The Divine Weeks and Works of Guillaume De Saluste Sieur Du Bartas.* Oxford: Clarendon.

Eschenbach, Wolfram von
- 1980 *Parzival.* Trans. A. T. Hatto. Harmondsworth: Penguin.

Evans, J. M.
- 1968 *"Paradise Lost" and the Genesis Tradition.* Oxford: Clarendon.

Faustbook, The
- 1592 *The Historie of the damnable life, and deserved death of Doctor Iohn Faustus.* Trans. P. F., Gent. London.

Frye, Northrop
- 1976 *The Secular Scripture: A Study of the Structure of Romance.* Cambridge: Harvard University Press.

Grotius, Hugo
- 1952 *Adamus Exul.* Trans. Kirkconnell, 1952:96-220.

Hoban, Russell
- 1980 *Riddley Walker.* London: Jonathan Cape.

Jung C. G.
    1953-79   *Collected Works*. Trans. R. F. C. Hull. 20 vols. London: Routledge and Kegan Paul.

Kane, Sean
    1981   "Spenser and the Frame of Faith." *University of Toronto Quarterly* 50:253-68.

Kingsley, Charles
    1863   *The Water-Babies, A Fairy Tale for a Land-Baby*. London: Macmillan.
    1876   *His Letters and Memories of His Life*. Ed. Frances E. Kingsley. 2 vols. London: Kegan Paul.

Kirkconnell, Watson
    1952   *The Celestial Cycle: The Theme of Paradise Lost in World Literature with Translations of the Major Analogues*. Toronto: University of Toronto Press.
    1973   *Awake the Courteous Echo: The Themes and Prosody of "Comus," "Lycidas," and "Paradise Regained," with Translations of the Major Analogues*. Toronto: University of Toronto Press.

Lacarrière, Jacques
    1977   *The Gnostics*. London: Peter Owen.

Landow, George P.
    1980   *Victorian Types, Victorian Shadows: Biblical Typology in Victorian Literature*. London: Routledge and Kegan Paul.

Le Goff, Jacques
    1988   "The Marvelous in the Medieval Imagination." Pp. 27-44 in *The Medieval Imagination*. Trans. Arthur Goldhammer. Chicago and London: University of Chicago Press.

Lessing, Doris
    1979   *Shikasta*. London: Jonathan Cape.

Lewalski, Barbara Kiefer
    1966   *Milton's Brief Epic: The Genre, Meaning and Art of "Paradise Regained."* Providence: Brown University Press.

Lewis, C. S.
    1943   *Perelandra*. London: John Lane, The Bodley Head.
    1950   *The Lion, the Witch and the Wardrobe*. London: Geoffrey Bles.
    1956   *Till We Have Faces*. London: Geoffrey Bles.
    1958   "Second Meanings." Chap. 12 in *Reflections on the Psalms*. London: Geoffrey Bles.

Lindsay, David
    1920   *A Voyage to Arcturus*. London: Methuen.

Lucretius (Titus Lucretius Carus).
    1966   *De Rerum Natura*. Trans. and intro. R. Latham as *On the Nature of the Universe*. Harmondsworth: Penguin.

MacDonald, George
    1858   *Phantastes, A Faerie Romance for Men and Women*. London: Smith, Elder.
    1871   *At the Back of the North Wind*. London: Strahan.
    1895   *Lilith, A Romance*. London: Chatto and Windus.

Manlove, C. N.
    1978   *Literature and Reality 1600-1800*. London: Macmillan.
    1992   *Christian Fantasy: From Twelve Hundred to the Present*. South Bend: University of Notre Dame Press.

Marlowe, Christopher
    1981   *The Tragicall History of Doctor Faustus*. In *Christopher Marlowe: The Complete Works*. Vol.2. Ed. Fredson Bowers. Second edition. Cambridge: Cambridge University Press.

Milton, John
    1968   *Paradise Lost*. In *The Poems of John Milton*. Ed. John Carey and Alastair Fowler. Longmans' Annotated English Poets. London: Longmans, Green.

Moorcock, Michael
    1969   *Behold the Man*. London: Allison and Busby.

Ovid (Publius Ovidius Naso)
    1955   *Metamorphoses*. Trans. Mary M. Innes. Harmondsworth: Penguin.

Paley, William
    1794   *A View of the Evidences of Christianity*. London: R. Faulder.
    1802   *Natural Theology*. London: R. Faulder.

Singer, Isidore, ed.
    1901-6   *The Jewish Encyclopaedia*. 12 vols. New York: Funk and Wagnalls.

Spenser, Edmund
    1912   *The Faerie Queene*. Book I, "The Legende of Holinesse." In *The Poems of Edmund Spenser*. Ed. J. C. Smith and E. de Selincourt. London: Oxford University Press.

Swedenborg, Emanuel
    1909   *Heaven and Hell*. Intro. J. Howard Spalding. London: J. M. Dent.

Tasso, Torquato
    1890   *Gerusalemme Liberata*. Trans. E. Fairfax and ed. H. Morley as *Jerusalem Delivered*. Carisbrooke Library VII. London: George Routledge.

Tolkien, J. R. R.
    1964   "On Fairy-Stories." Pp. 11-70 in *Tree and Leaf*. London: George Allen and Unwin.

Valvasone, Erasmo di
    1952   *L'Angeleida*. Translated sections in Kirkconnell 1952:80-7.

Virgil (Publius Vergilius Maro)
    1949   *The Fourth Eclogue*. In *The Pastoral Poems*. Trans. E. V. Rieu. Harmondsworth: Penguin.

Vondel, Joost van den
    1952   *Lucifer*. Translated sections in Kirkconnell 1952:361-421.

Whewell, William
    1840   *Philosophy of the Inductive Sciences*. London and Cambridge: John W. Parker and J. and J. J. Deighton.

Williams, Charles
    1931   *The Place of the Lion*. London: Gollancz.
    1945   *Descent into Hell*. London: Faber and Faber.

PROPHETIC AND APOCALYPTIC ESCHATOLOGY IN URSULA LE GUIN'S *THE FARTHEST SHORE* AND *TEHANU*

Mara E. Donaldson
Dickinson College

ABSTRACT

Prophetic and apocalyptic eschatology are themes found in contemporary women's fantasy literature. In fantasy new worlds and societies are explored; new eschatalogical visions are imagined. One prominent fantasy writer, Ursula Le Guin, uses biblical themes of the end of time in the imaginary worlds of her novels *The Farthest Shore* and *Tehanu*. Although the visions of hope differ in these novels, the essay argues that apocalypse as well as prophecy is a feminist alternative to the status quo.

1. Introduction.

Contemporary women's fantasy literature, like biblical prophecy and apocalypse, is a form of what Rosemary Jackson has called "the literature of subversion," a form of criticism of the social status quo. Like prophetic and apocalyptic literature, such fantasy is a popular genre, directed to ordinary people in the face of extraordinary circumstances. And like prophecy and apocalypse, women's fantasy offers an alternative view of the world as it might or ought to be.

P. D. Hanson (1975) has argued persuasively that whereas both prophecy and apocalypse are eschatological visions, they yet are distinguished by the forms of eschatological vision they announce. Contemporary women's fantasy literature is indebted to both of these forms of Jewish and Christian eschatology.

On the one hand, this fantasy literature is indebted to the tradition of Jewish *prophetic* literature, with its emphasis on social criticism aimed at those with the power to change the social order. Prophetic literature characteristically begins with words of denunciation of the current order, followed by the annunciation of doom, but almost always concludes by the promise of restoration, redemption or consolation. The prophetic tradition speaks from the perspective of the present and looks forward to an alternative, promised future.

On the other hand, women's fantasy literature is indebted to the traditions of Jewish and Christian *apocalyptic* literatures, with their emphasis on a radically alternative future for those currently disenfranchised. Apocalyptic literature characteristically begins with the revelation of the imminent end to the current order, and an *apokalypsis*, or unveiling of the alternative to the status quo, a glimpse of a future for those currently without any future.

This essay explores these prophetic and apocalyptic eschatological visions in two contemporary fantasies, *The Farthest Shore* and *Tehanu*, by Ursula K. Le Guin. At least since Rosemary Ruether (1983:22-23), feminist writers in religion have numbered among the "biblical resources for feminism" the "prophetic principle" of critique. However, the seeming otherworldliness and apparent dualism of apocalyptic have made feminists suspicious of its significance for post-patriarchal eschatologies. Apocalyptic has been condemned as one of those forms of "falsified religion at the right hand of oppressive political power" (27). Le Guin's fantasy novels—especially given the surprising appearance of a fourth volume to her Earthsea trilogy—provide an occasion to re-examine this now commonplace assumption about the apocalyptic tradition, particularly the issue of the role it plays in sustaining or criticizing the radical impropriety of injustice or evil in a good world.

2. *An Overview of the Earthsea Trilogy.*

Le Guin is one of the best known fantasy writers in America today, and her Earthsea books are among her most read fantasies. Originally imagined as a trilogy, the first volume, *A Wizard of Earthsea* was published in 1968. It begins the story of Ged, the young, impetuous mage, or wizard, who learns to use his skills wisely. It continues in *The Tombs of Atuan*, published in 1971, where Ged is now Archmage of Earthsea. Although Ged is a key character in *The Tombs*, the real hero of the story is Tenar, the girl-child chosen to be priestess of the Dark Ones.

The Earthsea trilogy apparently concluded in 1972 with the publication of *The Farthest Shore*. Here, Ged, now an old wizard, undertakes one final journey to restore order and balance to Earthsea. This he does with the help of a young warrior, Arren, son of the Prince of Enlad, who is destined to become a great king. In ultimately sacrificing his powers, Ged initiates a new era in Earthsea, the time once again of kings, fulfilling an eight century old prophesy.

Le Guin wrote about the trilogy in her essay "Dreams Must Explain Themselves" (1979:47-56). In the article, she gave every indication that *The Farthest Shore* was the last of her Earthsea books: "The book is still the most imperfect of the three, but it is the one I like the best. It is the end of the trilogy, but it is the dream I have not stopped dreaming" (1979:56). The subject of this third book is death; it is "about the thing you do not live through and survive" (1979:55).

Then, in 1990, Le Guin published *Tehanu*, which she subtitled *The Last Book of Earthsea*. Readers of the Earthsea books were perplexed. Why, when the Ged cycle seemed so nicely completed and the mantle passed to the young King Arren, write a fourth novel in what had been long conceived as a trilogy? What was so important to occasion *Tehanu*, in which the protagonist is not Arren, the young warrior king introduced in *The Farthest Shore*, but the woman Tenar, the hero of *The Tombs of Atuan*, and the girl-child Therru?

The resurrection of Earthsea and the shift in characters, however, are not the only striking characteristics of this novel. Its style is unlike that of the other novels and in fact is atypical of Le Guin's fantasy style more generally. The most striking example of the shift in style is seen early in the story. Tenar, now called Goha and a widow, adopts a young girl-child who has been severely beaten, burned, and abandoned. Fantasy literature, at least not the way most people understand "fantasy," does not usually deal with such realistic themes!

Like *The Farthest Shore*, *Tehanu* is about the end of an era and the beginning of a new one. This time, however, the new beginning involves the young child, Therru, who becomes the Tehanu of the title and eventually the first female mage, or wizard. For those familiar with Le Guin's fascination with balance and equilibrium, the fourth novel balances the second novel by finishing the story of Tenar. For others, it is a love story, consummating the love between Ged and Tenar at which the second novel only hinted. Still others have suggested that the novel answers Le Guin's feminist critics. These explanations, however, do not adequately account for the shift in style or character.

The reader schooled not only in fantasy literature but also in biblical literature will notice that *The Farthest Shore* and *Tehanu* offer strikingly different eschatological visions. *The Farthest Shore* is more prophetic in its eschatology; *Tehanu* is more apocalyptic in its vision of the end time. Thus, Le Guin challenges feminist readers, biblical scholars, and theologians to rethink the relationship between prophecy and apocalypse.

3. *Prophetic and Apocalyptic Eschatology.*

Prophecy and apocalypse are distinctive forms of eschatology; they provide two visions of a theology of hope. Hanson, who argues for a clear connection between prophecy and apocalypse, defines *prophetic* eschatology as

> the announcement to the nation of the divine plans for Israel and the world which the prophet has witnessed unfolding in the divine and which he translates into the terms of plain history, real politics, and human instrumentality. (1975:11)

Prophetic eschatology is this-worldly; its analysis of social deterioration is occasioned by the breakdown of the covenant relationship with Yahweh (Hos 14). It is addressed both to those who have power and to those who have abused power (Amos 2).

Yet its vision of hope for the new, transformed future is varied. For example, Amos speaks of a return to a purer Davidic time. "On that day I will raise up the booth of David that is fallen, and repair its breaches, and raise up its ruins, and rebuild it as in the days of old" (9:11). But Joel speaks of something brand new. "Then afterward I will pour out my spirit on all flesh; your sons and your daughters shall prophesy, your old men shall dream dreams, and your young men shall see visions (2:28). And Isaiah's words of hope seem to combine the two, speaking of a future that is both old and new. "A shoot shall come out from the stump of Jesse, and a branch shall grow out of his roots. . . . The wolf shall live with the lamb, the leopard shall lie down with the kid, the calf and the lion and the fatling together, and a little child shall lead them" (11:1, 6).

In contrast to the this-worldly focus of prophetic eschatology, apocalyptic eschatology is usually described as envisioning an other-worldly salvation, conditions in this world having deteriorated beyond repair. Hanson defines *apocalyptic* eschatology as

> the disclosure (usually esoteric in nature) to the elect of the cosmic vision of Yahweh's sovereignty—especially as it relates to his acting to deliver his faithful—which disclosure the visionaries have largely ceased to translate into terms of plain history, real politics and human instrumentality. (1975:11)

The words of apocalyptic discourse were addressed to those who were disenfranchised, those who were precisely the oppressed (Dan 3). Apocalyptic literature was an underground literature, written pseudonymously to encourage and strengthen those whose hope had been stripped away. It was an attack against the status quo, now so radically expressed that a vision of hope for the future could only be imagined as something beyond this world and its promises for salvation (Isa 24-27).

For example, Daniel begins to speak of the *resurrection* of the elect. "There shall be a time of anguish, such as has never occurred since nations first came into existence. But at that time your people shall be delivered, everyone who is found written in the book" (12:1). And the Apocalypse of John speaks of a "new heaven and a new earth," beyond all of conceivable creation. "See, I am making all things new," says the one on the throne (21:5). Thus, it is crucial to their distinctive theologies of hope that "*prophetic* eschatology centers on the history of Israel amid the nations of the world and points to a future *in* history with promises of a better life." But "*apocalyptic* eschatology looks beyond Israel to the cosmos, beyond the salvation of Israel to the final future *of* history itself" (Braaten:348, emphasis added).

4. *Fantasy: Apocalyptic and Subversion.*

The gift of biblical studies to fantasy literature is virtually self-evident. These different eschatologies—prophetic and apocalyptic—help us to notice the significance of the types of endings in Le Guin's final two Earthsea books. Without a knowledge of the biblical tradition, we would be incapable of understanding the significance of Le Guin's evolving ideas about the future.

What has not at all been obvious to students of biblical literature is the fashion in which fantasy literature has not merely *exemplified* or *illustrated* biblical genres, but has *enacted* them in the contemporary world in a way that the Bible itself sometimes no longer seems capable of doing. That is to say, fantasy literature at its best has provided occasions in which the biblical themes themselves become present cultural events. The prophetic emphasis on subversive social analysis and the apocalyptic intensification of the hope-that-is-promised both come to life in the form of the fantasy genre.

Writing in 1967, the year before Le Guin published *A Wizard of Earthsea*, Frank Kermode echoed the foreboding of many in America during that turbulent time, itself a sort of misplaced *fin de siècle*. "And of course we have it now, the sense of an ending" (98). Moreover, the link between those tempestuous cultural times and the biblical apocalypses became clear in works such as Hanson's *The Dawn of Apocalyptic*:

> To increasing numbers of observers it is becoming apparent that the dawn of a new apocalyptic era is upon us. . . . There is arising a profound disenchantment with the values and structures of our way of life. No longer does the optimism go unquestioned that ample education and hard work will be rewarded with all the benefits of the good life. (1975:1)

In the wake of the 1980s it has become hard to remember that for those who came of age during the 1960s and 1970s, the future would remain forever ambiguous. A whole generation could no longer take hope for granted. For many, this pessimism has persisted, their "teaching concerning the end of things" (Perrin: 121) having been transfigured at best into a hermeneutics of suspicion or deconstruction of modernity.

Peter Beagle, an impressive fantasy writer in his own right, might have had Hanson's comment in mind when he wrote:

> The sixties were the time when the word progress lost its ancient holiness and escape stopped being comically obscene. We are raised to honor all the wrong explorers and discoverers, thieves planting flags, murderers carrying crosses. Let us at last praise the colonizers of dreams. (Frontispiece)

Likewise, reflecting on the increased readership of Tolkien's fantasy trilogy, whose popularity peaked during the Vietnam War, Charlotte Spivack has argued that this interest was more than diversionary. "Much more than a mere best seller, *The Lord of the Rings* was a spiritual construct for our materialistic time, a powerfully evocative symbol of what seemed to be wrong and what should be done about it" (7). There was, we might say, a prophetic, if not apocalyptic, intent in Tolkien's fantasy.

For Spivack, Tolkien's significance lies in the element of "political subversion" she saw in his work, reminiscent of the great eighth-century prophets. "Tolkien converted the quest to *find something* into the quest to *destroy* something. As metaphor, Frodo's quest to destroy the ring of power signaled a protest against the establishment: antiwar, antitechnology, antipower politics" (7). In this project Tolkien followed the path on which earlier fantasies, such as Lewis Carroll's *Alice in Wonderland* or Frank Baum's *Wizard of Oz*, had embarked. However, in the case of Tolkien's work, "for the younger generation who read it twenty times, who memorized genealogies and learned to write Elvish, it had the force of a sacred text." Spivack concluded that it was a "devastatingly imaginative critique of our society" (7), a paradigm of what Rosemary Jackson has called "the literature of subversion." Rather than a sub-version of literature, a mere example of low-culture, fantasy subverts or undercuts the reader's everyday understanding of the world. It interrupts one's ordinary expectations with an implausible—W. R. Irwin would say "impossible"—alternative.

As Todorov states: "The fantastic is that hesitation experienced by a person who knows only the laws of nature, confronting an apparently supernatural event" (Todorov:25). Fantasy for Todorov involves a hesitation on the way to conviction. In the successful fantasy, the reader is brought up to the point of saying, "*I nearly reached the point of believing.*" In Todorov's view, "that is the formula which sums up the spirit of the fantastic. Either total faith or total incredulity would lead us beyond the fantastic: it is hesitation which sustains its life." Such hesitation must be experienced by the reader "as the first condition of the fantastic" (31), for when the hesitation ends, the fantastic becomes either "the marvelous" or "the uncanny," depending upon the way the reader resolves the question about the supernatural.

In fantasy, the "religious" dimension is not beyond, but within, this moment of hesitation and its ability to interrupt, and thus subvert, our expectations about the world. As political theologian Johann Metz concludes: "the shortest definition of religion [is] interruption" (171). Fantasy becomes "religious" by *narrating* the moment of hesitation itself. "Is narrative not the language of the interruption of the system—in other words, the language of the everything that eludes interpretation by our complex and metatheoretical systems of knowledge?" (Metz:215). Our argument here is that fantasy is itself the form *par excellence* of such narratives of interruption or subversion. It is within this perspective that we must now place Le Guin's two novels.

5. Prophetic Eschatology in *The Farthest Shore*.

All is not well in Earthsea. Mages, or wizards, have lost their skills, especially their ability to know the true names of things; crops fail, babies are sacrificed, and animals are born grossly deformed. The dragon Orm Embar tells Ged, "the sense has gone out of things. There is a hole in the world and the sea is running out of it. The light is running out. There will be no more speaking and no more dying" (1972:154). In short, the primary balance or equilibrium in Earthsea has been upset, and it is up to Ged, now an old wizard and archmage of Earthsea, and his young companion Arren to restore it.

Throughout the Earthsea stories Le Guin, deeply influenced by philosophical Taoism and Jungian psychology, makes equilibrium and identity cornerstones of her metaphysics. In *The Farthest Shore* the balance has been upset by a former wizard, Cob, who has discovered a way to cross the boundary between life and death. He returns to tempt villagers, witches, and other wizards with immortality, and the necessary balance between life and death is upset.

In order to restore balance, Ged uses all of his powers. When he and Arren finally follow Cob to Selidor, the source of the Dry River, "the place where a dead soul, crawling into earth and darkness, was born again dead" (1972:183), Ged closes the door. "Be thou made whole!" he said in a clear voice, and with his staff he drew in lines of fire across the gate of rocks a figure; the rune Agnen, the Rune of Ending" (1972:184). Yet in closing the door and finally releasing Cob from his life-in-death, Ged is no longer a mage, but a very weak man. It is up to Arren, and ultimately the great dragon Kalessin, to rescue them.

Arren is a curious character in the story. In some ways he reminds us of the young Ged, who goes to the School for Wizards on Roke Island to become a wizard, but who in his enthusiasm and impatience calls forth a shadow and also upsets the balance for a time. But Arren is not a wizard and does not come to Roke seeking Ged to become one. Instead, he is a young warrior, the son of the Prince of Enlad. He originally seeks Ged to tell him of the evil he has seen. He ends up staying and becoming the Archmage's companion on the journey to find the source of the imbalance.

Arren is the symbol of subversion in *The Farthest Shore*. He is the one who must learn the lesson that life and death balance one another; immortality upsets that balance. "To refuse death is to refuse life" (1972:121). Dying is the natural consequence of living. Ged tells Arren, "You will die. You will not live forever. Nor will any man nor any thing. Nothing is immortal. But only to us is it given to know that we must die. And that is a great gift: the gift of selfhood" (1972:122). His journey with Ged teaches him the lesson of mortality and makes him a good king. When at the end, as he struggles to carry an unconscious Ged out of the Dry Land, before Kalessin arrives, a very discouraged Arren finds a part of a rock from the Mountains of Pain. "He held it in his hand, the unchanging thing, the stone of pain. He closed his hand on it and held it. And he smiled then, a smile both somber and joyous, knowing, for the first time in his life, alone, unpraised, and at the end of the world, victory" (1972:191). As was the case with the mythic Gilgamesh, King of Uruk, all of the social and natural ills in *The Farthest Shore* have their origin in the quest for immortality. To subvert the "unnatural" longing for immortality is to root out the causes of injustice. Death "interrupts" life and in that way gives life its religious significance; Le Guin's fantasy narrates this subversion.

6. *Apocalyptic Eschatology in Tehanu.*

As mentioned above, *Tehanu* begins violently with the beating and burning of a young child. Tenar (or Goha), who had been the main character in *The Tombs of Atuan*, names this young child Therru, which means "burning, the flaming of fire" (1990:21). However, the violence against Therru is not the only brutality in the story. At the end, when Ged and Tenar are caught in a binding spell, Tenar is made to crawl like a dog, and she is beaten and kicked while Ged is left to watch.

The introduction of such graphic violence against women and children intensifies the social critique offered in the novel. With the violence done to both the child Therru and to Tenar, moral evil is added to the description of natural evil in *The Farthest Shore*. When Beech, the sorcerer of Valmouth, tried to lessen the pain and scarring of the burns on Therru, he said, "I think a time in which such things as this occur must be a time of ruining, the end of an age" (1990:15).

A year after Tenar saves Therru she is called to the bedside of the mage of Re Albi, Ogion. She takes Therru with her, for she is still in danger. When Ogion sees the scarred child he knows she is different. "That one—they will fear her." Tenar assumes he is referring to the way

Therru looks but that is not what the old mage means. Ogion says, "Teach her, Tenar... teach her all!" (1990:21)

There has never been a female mage in Earthsea. A hierarchical relationship exists between the male power of the mage and the female power of the witches of Earthsea. Witches could heal and prepare certain kinds of potions, but only mages knew the true names of things, and only the mages could truly change into another being. In referring to the untapped potential of female power, Auntie Moss, the witch of Gont, says, "No one knows, no one knows, no one can say what I am, what a woman is, a woman of power, deeper than the roots of trees, deeper than the roots of islands, older than the making, older than the moon" (1990:52).

Thus, the social criticism offered in *Tehanu* is directed particularly on behalf of women, those who are helpless and without real power. What is subverted here are the very foundations of male/female power that have sustained the Earthsea stories from the beginning.

7. *Conclusion: Fantasy—From Subversion to Hope.*

Popular fantasy is ultimately not only a subversive but also a hopeful genre. When it works well, the happy ending is also a new beginning. Le Guin's two visions of the happy ending in *The Farthest Shore* and *Tehanu* offer alternative readings of the future.

The first, *The Farthest Shore*, is more prophetic in its eschatology. The future is a logical extension of the themes begun in *The Wizard of Earthsea*. It is an example of the prophetic tradition's "this-worldly eschatology." In fulfilling an 800-year-old prophecy made by the last king, Arren returns the monarchy to Earthsea. He is the paradigm of hope understood as restoration of a glorious past, the fulfillment of a prophetic promise: "He shall inherit my throne who has crossed the dark land living and come to the far shores at the end of the day" (1972:17). *The Farthest Shore* both subverts our quest for immortality and offers a paradigm of hope as restoration.

The second, *Tehanu*, is more apocalyptic in its eschatology. It is an example of the apocalyptic tradition's "other-worldly eschatology." The best example of this is found in the story Tenar tells Therru of a time when there were beings who could be two things at once, both dragon and human. "They were all one people, one race, winged, and speaking the True Language. They were beautiful, and strong, and wise, and free" (1990:11). They did not remain one people, however. The dragons fled west and the humans settled on the land, and there was a constant fight between them.

The old story also told of some who remembered that they were both dragon and human, and some who fled not east but west. There, they live "in peace, great winged beings both wild and wise, with human mind and dragon heart" where,

> Farther west than west
> beyond the land
> [they] are dancing
> on the other wind. (1990:12)

Therru is one of these dragon-people. It is her destiny to usher in a new age for Earthsea, the age of the female mage. Thus, the hope that is offered is an authentically new beginning, something which has not been seen in Earthsea before.

In these two novels Le Guin challenges us to rethink the contributions biblical studies can offer contemporary feminist scholars. In contemporary feminist theologies, prophetic eschatology has until now provided the predominant vision of hope, as can be seen especially in the work of Letty Russell and Rosemary Ruether. The supposed superiority of prophetic eschatology is its this-worldliness over against the other-worldliness of apocalyptic.

Fantasy literature such as Le Guin's must be understood to share in such a this-worldly commitment, even when it draws upon the apocalyptic tradition. For the contribution of apocalyptic is not a shift away from this world to some other; it is the ability to sustain a hope for a radically new future. Like prophecy, apocalyptic offers a critique of the social status quo. But apocalyptic goes beyond prophetic hope in the radicality of its vision of the future. *Tehanu* allows us to reinterpret the seeming other-worldliness of apocalyptic as speaking not of justice beyond this world, but a world genuinely beyond injustice.

The productive tension between subversion and hope, therefore, is the central contribution of Le Guin's *The Farthest Shore* and *Tehanu*. We may say that both are fantasies because both subvert and redeem, but in different ways. *Tehanu* takes us beyond the prophetic eschatology of *The Farthest Shore* to apocalyptic eschatology. Its *subversion of injustice* is at the same time the beginning of an *enactment of promise*. In reading such fantasy literature, we are already beginning to journey "Farther west than west/beyond the land/[where] my people are dancing/on the other wind" (1990:9).

WORKS CONSULTED

Beagle, Peter S.
    1973   "Frontispiece." In J. R. R. Tolkien, *The Hobbit*. New York: Ballantine.

Braaten, Carl E.
    1985   "The Kingdom of God and Life Everlasting." Pp. 328-352 in *Christian Theology: An Introduction to Its Traditions and Tasks*. Eds. Peter C. Hodgson and Robert H. King. Second Edition. Philadelphia: Fortress.

Collins, John J.
    1974   "Apocalyptic Eschatology as the Transcendence of Death." Pp. 61-84 in *Visionaries and Their Apocalypses*. Ed. Paul Hanson. Philadelphia: Fortress.

Collins, John J., ed.
    1979   *Apocalypse: The Morphology of a Genre*. Semeia 14. Chico: Society for Biblical Literature.

Detweiler, Robert
    1990   "Apocalyptic Fiction and the End(s) of Realism." Pp. 153-183 in *European Literature and Theology in the Twentieth Century*. Eds. David Jasper and Colin Crowder. London: Macmillan.

Donaldson, Mara E.
    1990   "The Hero in Contemporary Women's Fantasy." *Listening: Journal of Religion and Culture* 252:140-153.

Hanson, Paul D.
    1975   *The Dawn of Apocalyptic*. Philadelphia: Fortress.

Hanson, Paul D., ed.
    1983   *Visionaries and Their Apocalypses*. Philadelphia: Fortress.

Irwin, W. R.
    1976   *The Game of the Impossible: The Rhetoric of Fantasy*. Urbana: University of Illinois Press.

Jackson, Rosemary
    1981   *Fantasy: The Literature of Subversion*. London: Methuen.

Kermode, Frank
    1967   *The Sense of an Ending: Studies in the Theory of Fiction*. London: Oxford University Press.

Le Guin, Ursula K.
    1968   *A Wizard of Earthsea*. Berkeley: Parnassus.
    1971   *The Tombs of Atuan*. New York: Atheneum.
    1972   *The Farthest Shore*. New York: Atheneum.
    1979   "Dreams Must Explain Themselves." Pp. 47-71 in *Language of the Night: Essays on Fantasy and Science Fiction*. Ed. by Susan Wood. New York: G. P. Putnam's Sons.
    1990   *Tehanu: The Last Book of Earthsea*. New York: Atheneum.

Lewis, C. S.
    1982   *On Stories and Other Essays on Literature.* Ed. Walter Hooper. New York: Harcourt Brace Jovanovich.

Manlove, Colin
    1975   *Modern Fantasy: Five Studies.* Cambridge: Cambridge University Press.

Metz, Johann Baptist
    1980   *Faith in History and Society.* Trans. David Smith. New York: Seabury.

Moltmann, Jürgen
    1967   *Theology of Hope: On the Ground and Implications of a Christian Eschatology.* New York: Harper & Row.
    1979   *The Future of Creation.* Philadelphia: Fortress.

Perrin, Norman
    1974   "Apocalyptic Christianity." Pp. 124-45 in *Visionaries and Their Apocalypses.* Ed. Paul Hanson. Philadelphia: Fortress.

Rabkin, Eric
    1976   *The Fantastic in Literature.* Princeton: Princeton University Press.

Ruether, Rosemary R.
    1983   *Sexism and God-Talk: Toward a Feminist Theology.* Boston: Beacon.

Russell, Letty M.
    1987   *Household of Freedom: Authority in Feminist Theology.* Philadelphia: Westminster.

Spivack, Charlotte
    1987   *Merlin's Daughters: Contemporary Women Writers of Fantasy.* New York: Greenwood.

Todorov, Tzvetan
    1973   *The Fantastic: A Structural Approach to a Literary Genre.* Translated by Richard Howard. Cleveland: Case Western Reserve University.

ADDITIONAL BIBLIOGRAPHY

Tina Pippin
George Aichele

Biblical scholars wishing to pursue fantasy theory and its relevance to the Bible may wish to consider the following works, in addition to those listed as "Works Cited" for the articles in this volume. Some works of special importance from the articles are again listed here to draw your attention to them.

Aristotle
  1967   *Poetics*. Trans. Gerald Else. Ann Arbor: University of Michigan Press.
Still immensely important for any consideration of literary theory. Aristotle does not directly address the topic of "fantasy," but his discussion of narrative, history, and philosophy is of direct relevance.

Attebery, Brian
  1980   *The Fantasy Tradition in American Literature from Irving to Le Guin*. Bloomington: Indiana University Press.
  1992   *Strategies of Fantasy*. Bloomington: Indiana University Press.
Attebery's main concern is with the newer theoretical models for reading fantasy literature. Fantasy is "mode, genre, formula" for Attebery; the categories of fantasy and science fiction and fiction overlap at points. Attebery explores postmodern fantasy and postmodern theory (Lance Olsen), along with feminist writings and theory and narratological concerns (story and character). He is heavily influenced by Tolkien.

Bachelard, Gaston
  1964   *The Poetics of Space*. Trans. Maria Jolas. Boston: Beacon.
  1969   *The Poetics of Reverie*. Trans. Daniel Russell. Boston: Beacon.
Bachelard's phenomenological studies have been largely ignored in North America; however, they have deeply influenced European scholars such as Barthes, Todorov, and Foucault.

Barr, Marlene S., ed.
  1981   *Future Females: A Critical Anthology*. Bowling Green: Bowling Green State University Press.
  1987   *Alien to Femininity: Speculative Fiction and Feminist Theory*. Westport: Greenwood.

Barthes, Roland
  1972   *Mythologies*. Trans. Annette Lavers. New York: Hill and Wang.
  1974   *S/Z*. Trans. Richard Miller. New York: Hill and Wang.

1975   *The Pleasure of the Text.* Trans. Richard Miller. New York: Hill and Wang.
1977   *Roland Barthes.* Trans. Richard Howard. New York: Hill and Wang.

Barthes does not write about fantasy as such, but nearly everything he wrote has profound implications for fantasy theory. He has greatly influenced Todorov and Kristeva.

Benjamin, Walter
1968   *Illuminations.* Trans. Harry Zohn. New York: Schocken.

Besides having a tremendous influence on Marxist scholars such as Zipes and Jackson, Benjamin's writings on narrative and technology are of great value to fantasy studies. Benjamin took fantasy seriously at a time when it was widely regarded as of little importance.

Bettelheim, Bruno
1989   *The Uses of Enchantment: The Meaning and Importance of Fairy Tales.* New York: Vintage.

An important psychoanalytic reading of the meaning of children's fairy tales and the effect of fantasy on our lives.

Bottingheimer, Ruth B.
1987   *Grimms' Bad Girls & Bad Boys: The Moral & Social Vision of the Tales.* New Haven: Yale University Press.

Bottingheimer, Ruth B., ed.
1986   *Fairy Tales and Society: Illusion, Allusion, and Paradigm.* Philadelphia: University of Pennsylvania Press.

Boyer, Robert H. and Kenneth J. Zahorski, eds.
1984   *Fantasists on Fantasy.* New York: Avon.

An excellent collection of theoretical writings on fantasy by fantasy writers themselves.

Brooke-Rose, Christine
1981   *A Rhetoric of the Unreal: Studies in Narrative and Structure, Especially of the Fantastic.* Cambridge: Cambridge University Press.

Develops and expands on Todorov's views, using a structuralist narratology.

Chatman, Seymour
1978   *Story and Discourse.* Ithaca: Cornell University Press.

Well-known book on narrative theory, with some important discussion of literary reference and the fantastic.

Cook, Elizabeth
1969   *The Ordinary and the Fabulous.* Cambridge: Cambridge University Press.

Cornillon, S. K., ed.
1972   *Images of Women in Fiction: Feminist Perspectives.* Bowling Green: Bowling Green State University Press.

Cox, Harvey
    1969   *The Feast of Fools*. Cambridge: Harvard University Press.

Duffy, Marleen
    1972   *The Erotic World of Faery*. London: Hodder and Stoughton.

Dunne, John S.
    1965   *The City of the Gods*. Notre Dame: University of Notre Dame Press.

Dunne and Cox are among a rather small number of contemporary theologians who draw in varying ways upon the fantastic. See also the works of Thomas J.J. Altizer, Mark Taylor, and David Tracy.

Farrer, Claire R., ed.
    1975   *Women and Folklore*. Austin: University of Texas Press.

Freud, Sigmund
    1955   "The 'Uncanny.'" Pp. 219-56 in *Complete Psychological Works*. Trans. Alix Strachey. Vol. 17. London: Hogarth.

An indispensable essay. Freud"s "uncanny" is essentially identical to Todorov's "fantastic."

Hume, Kathryn
    1984   *Fantasy and Mimesis: Responses to Reality in Western Literature*. New York: Methuen.

Hunter, Lynette
    1989   *Modern Allegory and Fantasy: Rhetorical Stances of Contemporary Writing*. London: Macmillan.

Irwin, W.R.
    1976   *The Game of the Impossible: A Rhetoric of Fantasy*. Urbana: University of Illinois Press.

Irwin and Hume are important fantasy theorists of the more traditional sort (fantasy as the polar reversal of reality). Hume's book is particularly strong on issues of reference.

Jackson, Rosemary
    1981   *Fantasy: The Literature of Subversion*. London: Methuen.

Jackson is (along with Jack Zipes) the foremost contemporary advocate of a Marxist view of literary fantasy. She is also sympathetic to Todorov's position and serves (with Brooke-Rose) as a bridge between the neo-Marxist and post-structuralist approaches to fantasy.

Koelb, Clayton
    1984   *The Incredulous Reader: Literature and the Function of Disbelief*. Ithaca: Cornell University Press.

Kreuziger, Frederick A.
    1982   *Apocalypse and Science Fiction*. Chico: Scholars Press.

Kristeva, Julia
- 1980   *Desire in Language.* Trans. Thomas Gora, Alice Jardine, and Leon S. Roudiez. New York: Columbia University Press.
- 1982   *Powers of Horror.* Trans. Leon S. Roudiez. New York: Columbia University Press.
- 1984   *Revolution in Poetic Language.* Trans. Margaret Waller. New York: Columbia University Press.
- 1987   *Tales of Love.* Trans. Leon S. Roudiez. New York: Columbia University Press.

Kristeva's development of a general theory of language and literature has been of great value to many fantasy scholars.

Lyotard, Jean-François
- 1984   *The Postmodern Condition: A Report on Knowledge.* Trans. Geoff Bennington and Brian Massumi. Minneapolis: University of Minnesota Press.
- 1988   *The Differend.* Trans. Georges Van Den Abbeele. Minneapolis: University of Minnesota Press.

Lyotard's work on language and conceptualization is very relevant to fantasy theory, and his 1984 book remains the most important statement on "postmodernism."

Magill, Frank N., ed.
- 1983   *Survey of Modern Fantasy Literature.* 5 vols. Englewood Cliffs: Salem.

Malmgren, Carl
- 1991   *Worlds Apart: Narratology of Science Fiction.* Bloomington: Indiana University Press.

Manlove, C.N.
- 1975   *Modern Fantasy: Five Studies.* Cambridge: Cambridge University Press.
- 1983   *The Impulse of Fantasy Literature.* Kent: The Kent State University Press.
- 1992   *Christian Fantasy: From Twelve Hundred to the Present.* South Bend: University of Notre Dame Press.

A very important contribution to contemporary theory from a largely "conservative" Tolkienian position.

Monleon, Jose B.
- 1990   *A Specter Is Haunting Europe: A Sociohistorical Approach to the Fantastic.* Princeton: Princeton University Press.

Moylan, Tom
- 1986   *Demand the Impossible: Science Fiction and the Utopian Imagination.* New York: Methuen.

Olsen, Lance
- 1987   *Ellipse of Uncertainty: An Introduction to Postmodern Fantasy.* New York: Greenwood.
- 1988   "Postmodern Narrative and the Limits of Fantasy." *Journal of the Fantastic in the Arts* 1:99–110.

Olsen has been the foremost explorer of links between the fantastic and the postmodern.

Palumbo, Donald, ed.
    1986   *Erotic Universe: Sexuality and Fantastic Literature.* New York: Greenwood.

Propp, Vladimir
    1968   *Morphology of the Folktale.* Ed. Louis Wagner and Alan Dunder. 2nd revised edition. Austin: University of Texas Press.

Rabkin, Eric S.
    1976   *The Fantastic in Literature.* Princeton: Princeton University Press.

Although working from a rather different set of presuppositions, Rabkin comes to conclusions much like Todorov's. Particularly useful for its attention to literary history.

Schlobin, Roger C., ed.
    1979   *The Literature of Fantasy: A Comprehensive, Annotated Bibliography of Modern Fantasy Fiction.* New York: Garland.
    1982   *The Aesthetics of Fantasy Literature and Art.* Notre Dame: University of Notre Dame Press.
    1985   "In the Looking Glasses: The Social and Cultural Fantasy Response." Pp. 3-9 in *The Scope of the Fantastic.* Westport: Greenwood.
    1990   "In Search of Creative Solitude: An Essay on the Fascination with Evil." *Journal of the Fantastic in the Arts* Summer:5-13.

Scholes, Robert
    1975   *Structural Fabulation: An Essay on the Fiction of the Future.* Notre Dame: University of Notre Dame Press.
    1979   *Fabulation and Metafiction.* Urbana: University of Illinois Press.

Serres, Michel
    1982   *The Parasite.* Trans. Lawrence R. Schehr. Baltimore: The Johns Hopkins University Press.

Shinn, Thelma J.
    1986   *Worlds within Women: Myth and Mythmaking in Fantastic Literature by Women.* Westport: Greenwood.

Siebers, Tobin
    1984   *The Romantic Fantastic.* Ithaca: Cornell University Press.

Spivack, Charlotte
    1987   *Merlin's Daughters: Contemporary Women Writers of Fantasy.* Westport: Greenwood.

Stewart, Susan
    1979   *Nonsense.* Baltimore: Johns Hopkins University Press.

Todorov, Tzvetan
    1975   *The Fantastic: A Structural Approach to a Literary Genre*. Trans. Richard Howard. Ithaca: Cornell University Press.
    1977   *The Poetics of Prose*. Trans. Richard Howard. Ithaca: Cornell University Press.
    1982   *Theories of the Symbol*. Trans. Catherine Porter. Ithaca: Cornell University Press.
    1990   *Genres in Discourse*. Trans. Catherine Porter. Cambridge: Cambridge University Press.

Todorov's structuralist theory of fantasy and his work on narratology and genres is a major influence on fantasy studies.

Tolkien, J. R. R.
    1963   "*Beowulf*: The Monsters and the Critics." Pp. 51-103 in *An Anthology of Beowulf Criticism*. Ed. Lewis E. Nicholson. South Bend: University of Notre Dame Press.
    1965   "On Fairy Stories." Pp. 3-84 in *Tree and Leaf*. Boston: Houghton.

Tolkien's "On Fairy Stories" is widely considered by fantasy writers and theorists to be the single most important statement on fantasy. The theological dimensions of this lecture/essay are also of considerable interest.

Walker, Nancy A.
    1990   *Feminist Alternatives: Irony and Fantasy in the Contemporary Novel by Women*. Jackson: University Press of Mississippi.

Wolfe, Gary K.
    1986   *Critical Terms for Science Fiction and Fantasy: A Glossary and Guide to Scholarship*. Westport: Greenwood.

Want a quick comparison of magic realism and fantasy? Feminist science fiction and eschatological romance? This guidebook is a good introduction to the terms and key theorists and writers in the field.

Wyatt, Jean
    1990   *Reconstructing Desire: The Role of the Unconscious in Women's Reading and Writing*. Chapel Hill: University of North Carolina Press.

Zipes, Jack
    1983   *Fairy Tales and the Art of Subversion: The Classical Genre for Children and the Process of Civilization*. New York: Methuen.
    1984   *Breaking the Magic Spell*. New York: Methuen.
    1991   *Spells of Enchantment: The Wondrous Fairy Tales of Western Culture*. New York: Viking Penguin.

www.ingramcontent.com/pod-product-compliance
Lightning Source LLC
Chambersburg PA
CBHW031317150426
43191CB00005B/264